THE CAMBRIDGE BIBLE COMMENTARY

NEW ENGLISH BIBLE

GENERAL EDITORS

P. R. ACKROYD, A. R. C. LEANEY, J. W. PACKER

GALATIANS

THE CAMBRIDGE BIBLE COMMENTARY

THE LETTER OF PAUL
TO THE
GALATIANS

COMMENTARY BY

WILLIAM NEIL

Warden of Hugh Stewart Hall,
University of Nottingham

CAMBRIDGE
AT THE UNIVERSITY PRESS
1967

Published by the Syndics of the Cambridge University Press
Bentley House, 200 Euston Road, London, N.W. 1
American Branch: 32 East 57th Street, New York, N.Y. 10022

© Cambridge University Press 1967

Library of Congress Catalogue Card Number: 66-29271

Printed in Great Britain
at the University Printing House, Cambridge
(Brooke Crutchley, University Printer)

GENERAL EDITORS' PREFACE

The aim of this series is to provide the text of the New English Bible closely linked to a commentary in which the results of modern scholarship are made available to the general reader. Teachers and young people preparing for such examinations as the General Certificate of Education at Ordinary or Advanced Level in Britain and similar qualifications elsewhere have been especially kept in mind. The commentators have been asked to assume no specialized theological knowledge, and no knowledge of Greek and Hebrew. Bare references to other literature and multiple references to other parts of the Bible have been avoided. Actual quotations have been given as often as possible.

Within these quite severe limits each commentator will attempt to set out the main findings of recent New Testament scholarship, and to describe the historical background to the text. The main theological content of the New Testament will also be critically discussed.

Much attention has been given to the form of the volumes. The aim is to produce books each of which will be read consecutively from first to last page. The introductory material leads naturally into the text, which itself leads into the alternating sections of commentary.

The series is prefaced by a volume—*Understanding the New Testament*—which outlines the larger historical background, says something about the growth and transmission of the text, and answers the question 'Why should we study the New Testament?' Another volume—*New Testament Illustrations*—contains maps, diagrams and photographs.

P.R.A.
A.R.C.L.
J.W.P.

CONTENTS

THE PROVINCE OF GALATIA

THE LETTER OF PAUL
TO THE
GALATIANS

✻ ✻ ✻ ✻ ✻ ✻ ✻ ✻ ✻ ✻ ✻ ✻ ✻

WHO WERE THE GALATIANS?

If you look at the map facing this page, you will see that the central part of Turkey around its capital Ankara was in Paul's day known as Galatia. The people who gave their name to the area had originally been Celtic tribesmen who had made their way from Europe into Asia Minor in the third century B.C. and founded a kingdom there. In 25 B.C. Galatia was made a province of the Roman Empire with its capital at Ancyra, now Ankara, but its boundaries were extended southwards to include not only the descendants of the original Celtic invaders but also other native peoples such as the Lycaonians, and various cities with a mixed population like those mentioned in the book of Acts: Iconium, Lystra, Derbe and Pisidian Antioch.

The narrative in Acts at this point (Acts 13–14) is concerned with Paul's first missionary tour, when with Barnabas and John Mark he set out from Syrian Antioch and sailed via Cyprus to Perga in the south of Asia Minor. From there they made their way northwards through the Taurus Mountains into the province of Galatia and arrived at Pisidian Antioch. The reason for this may well have been that Perga lay in a swampy area which brought on one of Paul's recurrent attacks of an illness that was in all probability malaria (Gal. 4: 13; 2 Cor. 12: 7).

John Mark left Paul and Barnabas at Perga, perhaps because he did not relish a trip into the backwoods of Asia

Minor. At all events he returned home to Jerusalem and the two older men went on, presumably when Paul had recovered and sought convalescence in the fresher mountain air to the north. Their route led them through Pisidian Antioch and Iconium where they conducted missions among Jews and Gentiles. Although they were hounded out of both districts, they successfully established little Christian communities before going on to the Lycaonian towns of Lystra and Derbe.

At Lystra they were among people whom civilized Romans would have called barbarians. They spoke their own native tongue instead of the normal colloquial Greek, which served as a common language throughout the Roman Empire, and they were simple and superstitious enough to mistake Paul and Barnabas for the gods Mercury and Jupiter come down to earth. Despite shocking ill-treatment, engineered by hostile Jews, Paul carried on with the mission, and having laid the foundations of a Christian congregation there and at Derbe the apostles retraced their steps, visiting each of the little communities again and organizing their leadership, before returning to the coast and thence by sea to their Syrian headquarters at Antioch.

North or South Galatia?

There are one or two other references in the book of Acts to Paul's later travels in Galatian territory (16: 6; 18: 23), and for all we know he may have founded other Christian churches on these occasions. If so, we do not even know where they were, and indeed we know little enough of the ones that have just been mentioned. But it seems most likely that it was to these four young Christian communities, founded on Paul's first missionary tour and subsequently visited again, that this letter was written. Barnabas, who was with Paul on that first campaign, is mentioned more than once in chapter 2 of the letter as if he were well known to the readers, and Paul's description of his first encounter with the Galatians in 4: 13–14 would seem to fit in well with the narrative of the first missionary tour in Acts 13–14. He refers to his illness at that time as having led to his campaign in that area, and when he reminds them that they welcomed him as if he had been 'an angel of God' it sounds like an allusion to Paul's initial reception at Lystra when he was greeted as Mercury, the messenger of the gods.

This view that the letter was written to the churches of South Galatia is relatively modern. Ancient commentators assumed that Paul was writing to the Celtic racial group living in North Galatia, the old geographical area of the Galatian kingdom before the Romans enlarged it into a province with a mixed population. Some modern scholars still support this view. But we know nothing about any churches having been founded by Paul in that part of the country, nor is it clear from the book of Acts when he could have visited the area, unless Acts 16: 6 and 18: 23 can be said to mean only the North and to exclude the South.

Moreover, Paul as a Roman citizen was in the habit of referring to groups of churches in terms of Roman provinces, as when he speaks of the congregations in Asia (1 Cor. 16: 19) and in Macedonia (2 Cor. 8: 1). It is therefore more than likely that when he addresses this letter to 'the Christian congregations of Galatia' (1: 2) he means the whole province. There are therefore very strong grounds for thinking of this letter as being addressed primarily in any case to the four little South Galatian Jewish–Gentile communities which were founded on Paul's first missionary journey as recorded in Acts 13–14.

WHY DID PAUL WRITE THIS?

No one has ever seriously doubted that Paul was the writer of this letter. What we know of the man and his mind from the letters to the Romans and to the Corinthians matches up perfectly with the contents of this 'great manifesto of Christian liberty'. The narrative of Paul's activities in the book of Acts connects at many points with the autobiographical details he

3

gives us in this letter. What we must ask, however, is: Why did he have to write to Galatia at all?

A quick glance at the letter will tell us at once that when Paul wrote it he was extremely annoyed. It begins abruptly without the usual friendly greetings, and at once it appears that the apostle is having to defend himself against charges which he is indignantly refuting. He accuses the Galatians of being stupid enough to be taken in by agitators who have been stirring up trouble, twisting the gospel into something quite different from what it ought to be, and casting aspersions on Paul himself. What was this all about?

It was indeed a serious matter and it was little wonder that Paul was furious. This letter takes us right to the heart of one of the great problems Christianity had to face in its early days, something that was far more crucial than merely the teething troubles of a growing young Church. Jesus and his disciples were Jews, racially of the same blood as Abraham, Moses, David, as well as the prophets and psalmists of Israel. Their homeland was the battle-scarred scene of more than a thousand years of Hebrew history; the Temple of Jerusalem and the local synagogues had moulded their religious upbringing; their Bible was the Old Testament.

It was only to be expected that, after the Crucifixion of Jesus, the Twelve Apostles, who became the leaders of 'the sect of the Nazarenes', as Christians were first commonly called (Acts 24: 5), regarded themselves as in every respect bound by the religious practices in which they had been brought up. Two thousand years of Jewish tradition were in their bones. The words of the Law and the Prophets which were their heritage were sacred and binding. Their association with Jesus had brought them to the conviction that he must be the long-promised Messiah for whom the Jews had hoped and prayed for centuries. Although this growing realization had often been difficult to square with what the Old Testament had said about Messiah, and was almost shattered when they saw the Messiah treated like a common criminal and

4

nailed upon a cross, the Resurrection and the appearances of the risen Christ finally convinced them that Messiah had indeed come and would soon return in power and judgement to found his Kingdom.

A gospel for Jews

This was the message they went out into the streets of Jerusalem to proclaim after the first Whitsunday. It was a call to their fellow Jews to accept this heaven-sent opportunity of getting into the right relationship with God through Christ and of becoming the People of God that Israel was meant to be, not merely by being born Jews but by being re-born in repentance, faith and obedience. Thus the invitation given by the Apostles to all Jews was to join the community of the new Israel, to share the new power of the Spirit which had come from Christ, enabling them to live in accordance with God's commandments, and to await the great day of Christ's Second Coming in full assurance of sharing in the blessings of his reign.

In all this there was no suggestion that those who accepted this invitation should be anything but orthodox Jews or that they should abate one whit of normal Jewish religious practice. The Temple and the Law of Moses were still supreme. The Good News was for the children of Abraham. If nothing had happened to change this attitude of the first Christian missionaries and force the young Church to restate its gospel in other terms, it is safe to say that Christianity would not have lasted for a generation. It would have flourished for a time as a Palestinian sect and died like so many others. For, stated in the terms in which the gospel was first proclaimed, it would have appeared to any intelligent pagan to be as absurd as it would appear to anyone today.

A gospel for the world

But Christianity was not destined to perish, and the whole narrative of the book of Acts is the story of how the Church was guided into an understanding that Christ came to renew the life of the whole world and not merely of his own race. As a result of this deeper insight the Church was forced to restate the gospel in terms that made sense to a pagan world which knew little and cared less about what went on in the Temple of Jerusalem or what was written in the Law of Moses.

When the Church came more and more to recognize that the gospel was a message of reconciliation between God and man, and between every man and his neighbour, and that the power of the Spirit of Christ was compelling it to break down every barrier of race, class and colour, it became obvious that it was not only a question of adopting new techniques of mission, or even of solving the problem of communicating Jewish ideas to a Gentile world, but that there had to be a radical rethinking of the whole relationship of Christianity to its Jewish origins. Within the confines of Jewry the Church could exist in association with Jewish orthodoxy. Jewish Christians had been brought up to believe that the ritual of the Temple, the practice of circumcision, the avoidance of contaminating paganism and abstention from certain types of food such as pork were all essential to salvation. This was the will of God as delivered to Moses and contained in the sacred Law.

What had Jesus said?

But could Gentiles be expected to treat these matters equally seriously? Were they of the essence of Christianity, or were they rather the stage props of its original setting which were no longer necessary when the next act of the drama had to be played against a different background? Further reflexion on Jesus' own attitude to Jewish practices made it apparent that while he was and indeed claimed to be the culmination of Old Testament hopes and prayers, he was highly critical not only of how the Old Testament was being interpreted in his day but also, on occasion, of the Old Testament itself.

Since his ministry was among Jews and since every Jewish male child was circumcised as a matter of course, Jesus had no cause to refer to this particular practice. But the sacred institution of the sabbath, by which the rabbis set so much store, he dismissed as being of less importance than human need (Mark 2: 27). He had mixed with the down-and-outs of society and broken through the caste system by including among his disciples a tax collector who trafficked with Gentiles (Mark 2: 13–17). He had trounced the scruples of the orthodox Jews who counted it sinful to eat 'unclean' food, by insisting that a man defiles himself by what he does and not by what he swallows (Mark 7: 17–23). His violent attack on the Temple traders cut at the roots of priestly practice and he shared the prophets' view that to love God and one's neighbour is worth more than the whole paraphernalia of animal sacrifice (Mark 11: 15–19; 12: 33–4). In the Sermon on the Mount he asserted his right not only to reinterpret the Law of Moses but to correct it (Matt. 5).

The 'God-fearers'

A contributory factor in helping the early Church to distinguish between what was of permanent and universal value in their Jewish heritage and what was merely a matter of racial upbringing and tradition, was the existence of groups of Gentile adherents of the Jewish synagogues in the cities and towns of the Roman Empire. These 'God-fearers', as they were called, were serious-minded pagans who found no satisfaction in the various religious cults of the day but were attracted to the beliefs and practices of the Jews who lived in their midst. They were attracted by a faith which maintained that there is only one God and by the high standards which were proclaimed in the synagogues which they attended as sympathetic worshippers. It was open to any and all of them to become converts to the Jewish religion, and Jewish missionary propaganda was directed actively to win them over. Most of them, however, were unwilling to take this step, since it involved among other things full compliance with Jewish Law, including circumcision, abstention from prohibited food and avoidance of social contact with their Gentile neighbours.

The last of these requirements would virtually involve joining the Jews in their self-imposed isolation from the rest of the community, the second was full of practical difficulties in a normal pagan city, but the first above all was the ultimate deterrent. To the average citizen of the Roman Empire who had learned from the Greeks to appreciate the beauty of the human body, the idea of mutilating it by circumcision appeared revolting and barbaric—apart from being extremely painful. Devout adherents of the synagogue could see no connexion between the austere God of the Old Testament prophets and the high morality of the Ten Commandments on the one hand, and this relic of oriental tribalism on the other. However the rabbis might explain circumcision as the outward sign of an inward commitment to God, most pagan sympathizers preferred to retain the status of adherents.

The impact of Stephen

There was thus a pattern and a precedent in Judaism outside Palestine which did not fail to influence the policy of the early Church when it moved outward from its original setting in Jerusalem to the cosmopolitan cities of the empire. Even before this happened there was a cleavage of opinion among the Jewish Christians of Jerusalem: between those who regarded the new faith as an improved form of Judaism of the narrower type and those who had begun to see that Judaism and Christianity could no more be mixed together than oil and water. Particularly, this would seem to have been the case with those Jewish Christians who had lived outside Palestine and who knew the more liberal practice of the synagogues overseas in accepting as useful adherents pagans who refused to accept what conservative Palestinian-born Christians would have held to be as essential to Christianity as to Judaism.

The chief protagonist of this point of view was Stephen,

8

whose defence of it ended in his martyrdom. From the account of him given in Acts 6 and 7 he appears to have been a brilliant advocate of the difference between Christianity and Judaism, emphasizing the importance of observing the spirit of the Old Testament as opposed to the letter. He insisted that the People of God, as the Jews claimed to be, did not depend upon the sacred soil of Palestine or the holy Temple of Jerusalem or the rite of circumcision. By implication, of course, if these things were not important for Jews they were even less important for Christians. Stephen constitutes a half-way stage between the original conservatism of the Twelve Apostles and the radical attitude of Paul on the question of how far the Church should be anchored to its Jewish foundations.

Gentiles: second-class Christians?

Stephen's bold critique of Judaism led to the first persecution of the Christians, in which a foremost part was played by the zealous rabbi Saul of Tarsus. But it was, in the purpose of God, this very persecution that enabled Christianity to become a world religion, not least through the efforts of the same Saul after his conversion. Driven from Jerusalem, the Christian gospel was planted in one town after another throughout Palestine and Syria. Wherever the Christians went they proclaimed their faith, and it was not long before Gentiles were clamouring to be admitted to the fellowship of the Church. On what terms were they to be admitted? Was the Church to follow the pattern of Judaism and have two levels of association—full membership for those who had been brought up as Jews or were prepared to become Jews by acceptance of the Old Testament Law, including circumcision, and second-class status as adherents for Gentile Christian 'God-fearers' who were willing to acknowledge Jesus Christ as Lord but unwilling to enter his Church if it involved becoming Jews in order to do so?

Paul's view of the Church

Whatever reservations the Twelve Apostles and the conservative Jerusalem Christians may have had, and however
reluctant they may have been to face up to the issue, it was the
unwavering belief of Paul, held with passionate conviction,
that Christ had broken down the barrier between Jews and
Gentiles and that there must be no second-class citizens
within his Church.

As a 'Hebrew born and bred', as he called himself (Phil.
3: 5), no one believed more than Paul in the priceless legacy
that had been entrusted to Israel and that was now the
inheritance of the Church, the revelation of God's nature and
purpose contained in Old Testament scripture. No one
believed more than Paul that Christ and his Church were the
fulfilment of God's promises to his ancient people the Jews;
no one believed more in the special role that Jews had still
to play in God's plan for the salvation of the world. As a
loyal son of the traditions of his race, Paul regarded it as right
and proper for himself and all other Jewish Christians to
respect the religious and social practices in which they had
been brought up. His aim was that Jews should become Jewish
Christians, not that they should cease to be recognizable as
Jews. For them circumcision was still an obligation, the
Temple of Jerusalem and all that went on in it was still the
focus of their worship.

But he was equally convinced that none of this was
necessary for salvation, still less that it applied to Gentiles. In
their case commitment to Christ and baptism were all-
sufficient and gave them equal status with Jewish Christians
in the new Israel of God, the Church. He resisted consistently
and utterly any attempt on the part of Jewish Christians to
force non-Jews to be circumcised or to be burdened by
obligations to keep Jewish ceremonial law. His argument, as
we shall see in this letter, was simply that Christ had made men
free of all such external regulations. The right relationship

with God was open to Jew and Gentile alike. As far as Gentiles were concerned this was possible through faith alone and not by observance of Old Testament ordinances, however hallowed and venerable they might be.

Circumcision or faith

Paul's attitude in the matter was a mixture of sound politics and theological conviction. Outside Palestine, in the pagan world, Christianity made its biggest impact upon the Gentiles via the fringe adherents of the Jewish synagogue. To these people, already familiar with the Old Testament faith, Christianity made an even stronger appeal than Judaism. It preserved all that had attracted the pagan adherents to the synagogue in the first place, a monotheistic faith with a strong moral content, but as it was presented by Paul and his associates it was no longer bound up with Jewish exclusiveness or saddled with built-in Jewish restrictive practices.

If Paul had not fought tooth and nail for the right of Gentiles to by-pass circumcision, food taboos and the like, there would have been little in Christianity to woo the 'God-fearers' away from the synagogues. To them Christianity would simply have been the old mixture with a different label, and their vital role as a bridge between the Jewish and the pagan world would have gone by default.

But deeper than this practical issue was the apostle's underlying conception of the unity of the Church. It must be one Body of Christ, not divided into a Jewish section and a Gentile section; and in that one Body every part was of equal value in the sight of God.

Paul faces the problem

Here then is the key to this letter, which explains why it is written with such vehemence and passion. What had obviously happened was that in the apostle's absence some fanatics had been busily at work among the little congregations in Galatia claiming that no Gentile could call himself a proper Christian unless he first became a Jew by submitting to circumcision and accepting the obligations of Jewish Law. For good measure they had been questioning Paul's credentials. Was he not after all an upstart without real authority? The true leaders of the Church were the Twelve Apostles. It was they who had been appointed custodians of the faith, not this ex-rabbi who was prepared to jettison the tradition of a thousand years by admitting Gentiles to full membership of the New Israel without regard to the commandments of God in his sacred Law.

Whether the trouble-makers were Jewish Christians or Gentile converts to Judaism who had become more Jewish than the Jews is not of great importance. What Paul is concerned about in this letter is his right to speak in the name of Christ by virtue of his direct commission at his conversion on the Damascus road, without a delegated authority from the Jerusalem hierarchy. More vital still, the sole qualification for full membership of the Christian Church is commitment to Christ, with baptism as its outward symbol. Whether a man has been brought up as a Jew or a Gentile is irrelevant. Life, as life is meant to be lived, with purpose, hope and meaning, has now been made available to every man through Christ. The Law of Moses has served its turn. Faith in Christ is now all that matters.

WHEN WAS THIS LETTER WRITTEN?

Scholars have argued for placing this letter at almost every stage of Paul's ministry, ranging from the claim that this is the earliest of his letters to the suggestion that it might be one of his last. The answer depends to some extent on whether we reckon that he was writing to the unknown congregations of North Galatia or to the churches in South Galatia referred to in Acts as having been founded on his first missionary journey. If it was to the former group, the letter cannot have been written before his visits to the 'Galatian country', referred to in Acts 16: 6 and 18: 23. In this case the most

12

likely date would be some time during his third missionary enterprise while he was working at Ephesus (A.D. 53–56).

If we are right in thinking that he was writing primarily to the Christians of South Galatia in such places as Pisidian Antioch, Iconium, Derbe and Lystra (Acts 13–14), it still does not settle the matter. Since on his first missionary tour he paid two visits to these towns and appears to refer in this letter to two previous missions (4: 13), it could have been written any time after then. But when? The most likely answer would be—'Very soon, and certainly before the council of Jerusalem.' According to the narrative in Acts— and there is no reason to suppose that it is not reliable—when Paul and Barnabas returned to their base at Antioch in Syria after the first missionary tour, they found themselves in the middle of a crisis over the very question that forms the subject of this letter, namely the terms on which Gentiles could be admitted to the Church.

The Council of Jerusalem

In their absence the advocates of the narrow Jewish-Christian view that circumcision was essential to salvation had caused so much trouble and confusion in the church at Antioch that it was decided that Paul and Barnabas, as representatives of the more liberal attitude, should go to Jerusalem and try to reach some understanding with the apostles and other Church leaders. This Council of Jerusalem, described in Acts 15, is usually dated at A.D. 49. It was a victory for Paul and the liberals. Apart from some minor reservations the Council agreed that full membership of the Church should be open to Gentiles without requiring them to conform to Jewish Law, in particular the obligation of circumcision. This decision was embodied in a decree, armed with which Paul and Silas were able to visit the Galatian congregations again, among others, and to reassure them with this authoritative ruling from Jerusalem.

It is extremely unlikely that Paul would have written this

letter, in which he is at such pains to argue the case for admitting Gentiles without forcing them to submit to the demands of Jewish Law, if he had had this trump card in his hand. The letter must therefore have been written before the Council of Jerusalem, say in A.D. 48, and would in that case be the earliest of Paul's letters as we have them in the New Testament. It would then have been written from his base at Syrian Antioch or on his way to the Council, when word was presumably brought to him that the good foundations which he had laid in Galatia during the first missionary journey were being undermined by these Judaizers.

Other views

Many scholars would dissent from this view, on the grounds that Acts is not historically reliable, and that since Galatians has so much in common both in thought and style with the major Pauline letters which were written during his third missionary campaign, namely Romans and 1 and 2 Corinthians, it is more properly dated about the same time, say A.D. 55, and was most likely written from Ephesus. Another suggestion is that the letter may have been written during Paul's imprisonment in Rome between A.D. 59 and 61. Although there is no mention of prison in this letter, it is held that if he had not been in captivity the grave situation in the Galatian churches would surely have sent him hurrying there to put things right.

Against this it could be argued that if he got the bad news from Galatia and immediately wrote this letter while he was actually on his way to the Council of Jerusalem, he might well have thought it more important to get an official decision as soon as possible than to tackle the problem by a visit to Galatia which might have no more effect than a letter. As for the similarity of thought and style between this letter and Romans and 1 and 2 Corinthians, suggesting that all were written at about the same time (A.D. 53–6), it is surely not impossible that Paul would be as likely to use the same phraseology in A.D. 48 as he would in A.D. 55, especially if he is dealing with the same subject, as is the case in Romans and Galatians.

A.D. 48 or 49

The view taken in this commentary is (a) that we can rely on Acts as being basically a historical record, and the work of Luke, Paul's medical missionary companion, (b) that the narrative of Acts can be squared with Paul's autobiographical information in Galatians, and (c) that consequently the best solution of the problem of dating the letter is to place it between Paul's first double visit to Galatia (as recorded in Acts 13–14) and the Council of Jerusalem (described in Acts 15). It can therefore be dated A.D. 48 or 49.

WHAT DOES THE LETTER SAY?

One of the reasons for studying any book of the Bible seriously and with the help of a commentary, is to find out what, if anything, it still has to say to us in the twentieth century. Obviously some parts of the Bible will appear at once to have more relevance to present-day life than others. But in practically every case we are up against the difficulty that the background, thought-forms, vocabulary and so on belong to a different age. At no time since the Church was founded has this been more keenly felt than in the present century. Yet, as soon as we begin to make the effort to find out what lies behind the particular words and ideas which at first sight seem so remote from our time, it becomes clear that behind this discouraging scaffolding lie vital issues that still confront us, as well as satisfying answers to the questions that still perplex us.

But we nevertheless have to begin with the spadework, which consists in finding out how a particular writer in his own day expressed his ideas and convictions about the meaning of life in terms of the particular situation in which he found himself. It may well seem, for example, that nothing could be more irrelevant for our time than a letter like this, which deals primarily with ritual circumcision and with Jewish legalism in general. Yet it is only by dealing with the concrete situation as it affects people's lives that a writer of the calibre of Paul can convey the timeless truths that he has grasped so much more clear-sightedly than we. We must therefore ask ourselves first what this letter says in terms of its own day before trying to translate it into terms that fit ours.

1: 1–24   *Paul's unique commission*

After a lukewarm greeting to the congregations in Galatia, Paul without more ado accuses them of having betrayed the gospel as he had taught it by listening to people who were twisting it into something different. What he had brought them was no second-hand message. He had received it from Christ himself. He recalls how before his conversion to Christianity no one had been a more fervent upholder of Jewish tradition than he had been, and no one had worked harder to wipe out the new Christian heresy. Then God laid his hand on him and commissioned him to become an apostle to the Gentiles of the faith he had tried to destroy.

He embarked on this task without permission, authorization or even consultation with any of the leaders of the Church at its Jerusalem headquarters. He did not even meet Peter until three years later, when he stayed with him in Jerusalem for a couple of weeks to get to know him. The only other Christian dignitary he met on that occasion was James, the brother of Jesus. For the next several years he was working as a missionary on his own in Syria and Cilicia.

2: 1–21   *Apostle to the Gentiles*

Only after fourteen years did he visit Jerusalem again. This time he took with him Barnabas and Titus. He had an opportunity then to discuss with the Church leaders the kind of line he had been taking in his mission among the Gentiles. At that meeting there was no suggestion that Titus, a Greek, should be circumcised, nor had the Church leaders any hesitation in admitting at once that Paul was as surely commissioned by God to be the apostle of Christ's gospel to the Gentiles as Peter had been similarly entrusted with the task of proclaiming it to the Jews. On that occasion Barnabas and Paul had been accepted as equals by James, Peter and John, and had returned to work among the Gentiles with their blessing. Nothing more was asked of them than that they should bear in mind the poverty-stricken Christian community in Jerusalem.

What was more, Paul had a little later had what we should call a 'show-down' with Peter himself. The chief apostle had come to Antioch, the centre of Gentile Christianity, where Paul was in charge, and had been quite happy to mix freely with the Gentile Christians until some of the stricter Jewish Christians from Jerusalem appeared on the scene and protested. Then Peter and even Barnabas took fright and conformed to the ultra-conservative policy of religious separatism. It was at this point that Paul took Peter to task in front of the whole congregation. He made it plain to him that he could not have it both ways. 'If it was all right for you', he said to Peter, 'born and bred as a Jew, to live so recently like a Gentile, what right have you to expect Gentiles to follow the Jewish pattern of life?'

What makes a man right with God is faith in Christ, not compliance with the regulations imposed by Jewish Law. If Jews who have become Christians are now guilty of offences against the Law this does not make them sinners. The sin would be to try to bolster up a system which is now inadequate and out of date. Paul had himself tried to find salvation through the Law and had failed. He knew now that it could come only through commitment to Christ, by dying to the past and rising again to new life in Christ and his Church. If the way to God lay through observing the letter of the Law and not through Christ, there would have been no meaning in Jesus' death.

3: 1–29   *Faith or Law*

Paul now challenges his Galatian readers. Did all their rich experience as Christians, and all the evidence they had seen of the Holy Spirit at work among them, come to them because they observed Jewish Law or because they believed the gospel message? Even Abraham, the father of the Jewish people, found favour with God because he was a man of faith. So the true sons of Abraham are not those who are his racial descendants but those who share his faith in God. It is by faith that men obtain God's blessing, not by trying to comply with the impossible demands of the Law. Indeed we are told in the Law itself that anyone who fails to keep the Law is under a curse. But Christ did not keep the Law. He broke it by dying upon a cross which according to the Law put him also under a curse. What he has therefore done is to free us from the curse under which we all stand through failing to keep the Law, by taking it upon his own shoulders. So the way is open for Gentiles and Jews alike to live now by the power of the Spirit.

The promise of God's blessing to Abraham included Christ and all who commit themselves to him. It could not be affected by the Law of Moses, which came several centuries later. The Law was simply a temporary guardian of the life of the People of God until Christ should come. When Christ came the way was open for all, Jews and Gentiles, free citizens and slaves, men and women, to become part of one great fellowship united to Christ and to one another.

4: 1 — 5: 1   *Freedom or slavery*

Before Christ came we were all alike at the mercy of fate. But Christ by defeating the power of the Law has freed us from its restraints and made it possible for us to become the sons of God that we were meant to be. Our own experience of God assures us that he is dealing with us as a Father with his children and not as a tyrannical master with his slaves. How can you then, says Paul to the Galatians, go back on this and return to slavish observance of religious rules and regulations?

Paul then reminds his readers of his first visit to them and the happy relationship that existed between them. Is all this forgotten because of these trouble-makers who want to rob them of their freedom and force them back under the yoke of the Law? Surely the Scriptures make it plain in the story of Abraham that in the relationship between the sons of his true wife and of his slave-woman, we can see an allegory of the relationship between the slavery of Judaism and the freedom of Christianity. Christians are, like Isaac, born into the liberty of true sonship.

5: 2–25   Liberty not licence

To submit to circumcision means turning your back on Christ, continues the apostle, and means saddling yourself with the burden of keeping the whole of the Law. The life of a Christian is built on an entirely different foundation—on faith and love. In this kind of relationship between God and man circumcision makes no difference one way or the other, and whoever is trying to persuade the Galatians that it does will have to answer to God.

There is, however, another danger which must be guarded against, namely, to confuse Christian freedom with licence. If his readers will let the Spirit of God rule their lives they will find that they will be helped to avoid the wrong kind of behaviour and to respond to God's love for them with a Christ-like love for one another.

5: 26 — 6: 18   Love in action

The Christian life also involves humility in ourselves and forgiveness of the mistakes of others. We reap what we sow, whether it is good or evil. Let us never lose heart in working for the whole community, above all for the Church. These enthusiasts for circumcision are bogus. They only want to be able to boast that they have won their case. But, as for me, concludes Paul, the only thing I want to boast about is the cross of Christ which has made me a changed man and this has nothing to do with whether I am circumcised or not.

So calling on God to bless all who see that this is the heart of the whole matter, an Israel of God, embracing Jew and Gentile, and reminding his readers of what he has suffered in promoting it, Paul ends with a farewell grace.

Having given this quick look at the contents of the letter, we can see why the editors of the New English Bible have suggested as its sub-title *Faith and Freedom*. For apart from the autobiographical section at the beginning and the practical instructions at the end, the chief theme of the letter is that Christianity is a religion that makes us free, and that this happens when we come into the right relationship with God through Christ, the relationship being faith. What is equally obvious, however, is that to make a bald statement of this kind raises—or ought to raise—a host of questions in our minds. What does Paul mean by freedom? What are we freed from? What are we freed for? How do we come into the right relationship with God and what has Christ got to do with it? Clearly a quick glance at the contents is not enough, and what we must do now is to look more closely at the letter itself and come to grips with Paul's argument, before we are in a position to say what it all means in terms of the twentieth century.

✵   ✵   ✵   ✵   ✵   ✵   ✵   ✵   ✵   ✵   ✵   ✵   ✵

Faith and Freedom

I: I-24 PAUL'S UNIQUE COMMISSION

PAUL'S OPENING GREETING

FROM PAUL, an apostle, not by human appointment or **1** human commission, but by commission from Jesus Christ and from God the Father who raised him from the dead. I and the group of friends now with me send **2** greetings to the Christian congregations of Galatia.

Grace and peace to you from God the Father and our **3** Lord Jesus Christ, who sacrificed himself for our sins, to **4** rescue us out of this present age of wickedness, as our God and Father willed: to whom be glory for ever and **5** ever. Amen.

✢ Compared with the opening words of other Pauline letters, this is a distinctly chilly beginning. Paul is essentially a father in God to all the young churches, yet here are none of the usual encouraging words of praise or of gratitude to God for their good work. The reason becomes apparent in the next paragraph, but there is already a hint of it here in what is left unsaid. Paul's indignation is obvious right from the start.

1. The word *apostle*, which means a messenger, is generally used in the New Testament to refer to the twelve disciples who were originally sent out by Jesus to preach the gospel and to heal the sick. When the Church began to take shape after the death of Jesus, the Twelve were regarded as the final authority in all matters of faith and practice. By this time Judas Iscariot had been replaced by Matthias (Acts I: 26). It is clear from Paul's letters, however, that already in the early days the word 'apostle' was being more widely used (I Cor. 15: 7). Paul generally speaks of himself as an 'apostle of Jesus Christ'.

Here he is emphasizing that he is a messenger of the gospel, not because he has been authorized or commissioned by the Twelve or by any other person but by Christ himself. He points to the moment of his conversion as giving him the right to call himself an apostle. It was then, in his encounter with the risen Christ, after God had *raised him from the dead*, that he was set apart for his life's work. The implication is, of course, that it was being said that he was not a real apostle because he had not been commissioned by Jesus as the Twelve had been. His reply is that his commission was also from Jesus and that this gave him equal status with them.

2. The fact that Paul speaks of *the group of friends now with me* suggests a small party rather than a whole congregation. This would fit in with the idea that Paul wrote this on the way to the Council of Jerusalem (see p. 14).

There may be other *Christian congregations of Galatia* included in the greeting apart from the four mentioned in Acts 13–14, namely Pisidian Antioch, Iconium, Lystra and Derbe, but we can assume that it is primarily to these four that the apostle is writing.

3–5. We could paraphrase as follows: 'Grace and peace to you from God the Father and our Lord Jesus Christ, who lived and died in such perfect conformity with the will of God that by identifying ourselves with him we can begin to live here and now in the right relationship to God as we shall know it more fully hereafter.' ✳

A TRAVESTY OF THE GOSPEL

6 I am astonished to find you turning so quickly away from him who called you by grace, and following a different 7 gospel. Not that it is in fact another gospel; only there are persons who unsettle your minds by trying to distort the 8 gospel of Christ. But if anyone, if we ourselves or an angel from heaven, should preach a gospel at variance

with the gospel we preached to you, he shall be held outcast. I now repeat what I have said before: if anyone 9 preaches a gospel at variance with the gospel which you received, let him be outcast!

Does my language now sound as if I were canvassing 10 for men's support? Whose support do I want but God's alone? Do you think I am currying favour with men? If I still sought men's favour, I should be no servant of Christ.

✶ Paul maintains that there is only one version of the gospel and that is the one the Galatians had heard from him during his mission. It was a basic part of the Good News according to Paul that Jews and Gentiles alike could become Christians on equal terms. Now the Galatians were being asked to believe something different. This, as we learn later in the letter, was that Gentiles must first become Jews before they can become Christians.

6. *so quickly:* this seems to imply that the letter is being written not long after the original missionary campaign.

In Paul's view the fundamental truth about Christianity is that it is a religion of *grace* and not of merit. That is, that we come to a right relationship with God not by priding ourselves on complying with rules about how we should behave but by responding to his love. It is his power that enables us to live the kind of life we were meant to live, in harmony with God and our fellow men.

7. The trouble-makers in the Galatian churches were suggesting that the right relationship with God was only possible if certain rules were observed, such as circumcision, restricted diet and so on. This attempt to acquire merit in the sight of God is described by Paul as a distortion of the gospel, not Good News at all but bad news.

8–9. Paul had apparently had reason before to warn the Galatian churches not to listen to these people who were perverting the gospel. Now he trenchantly denounces them. *Outcast* (Greek: *anathema*) means either 'accursed' or, as the N.E.B. translation suggests, 'banned from the community'.

10. Paul is also apparently being accused of being a time-server, running with the (Gentile) hares and hunting with the (Jewish) hounds in order to win converts at any price. He said himself elsewhere that he tried 'to meet everyone half-way' (I Cor. 10: 33), a policy which is always open to attack and misunderstanding. Whatever he does, he says here, is done in the service of Christ. His personal popularity is the last thing he is concerned about, otherwise he would not be writing to the Galatians in such strong terms. ✻

PAUL'S CONVERSION

11 I must make it clear to you, my friends, that the gospel
12 you heard me preach is no human invention. I did not take it over from any man; no man taught it me; I received it through a revelation of Jesus Christ.

13 You have heard what my manner of life was when I was still a practising Jew: how savagely I persecuted the
14 church of God, and tried to destroy it; and how in the practice of our national religion I was outstripping many of my Jewish contemporaries in my boundless devotion
15 to the traditions of my ancestors. But then in his good pleasure God, who had set me apart from birth and called
16 me through his grace, chose to reveal his Son to me and through me, in order that I might proclaim him among the Gentiles. When that happened, without
17 consulting any human being, without going up to Jerusalem to see those who were apostles before me, I went off at once to Arabia, and afterwards returned to Damascus.

* Paul is saying here that the message he proclaimed in Galatia—that membership of the Church was open to all who were prepared to commit their lives to Christ, irrespective of whether they had been brought up as Jews or Gentiles—could not possibly have been thought up by himself or indeed by anybody else. No one was less likely than he, the most devoted upholder of Jewish tradition before his conversion, suddenly to proclaim the unimportance of all this for the Christian life unless it had come to him as a revelation from God. And, indeed, says Paul, this is just what happened on the Damascus road when Christ took hold of him (Phil. 3: 12). When this shattering experience convinced him how wrong he had been to persecute the followers of Christ, he made no move at all to contact the leaders of the Church, but went off by himself to work out what it all meant. He needed no authorization from the Twelve. God himself had made him an apostle of Christ.

12. We should be clear that when Paul says that *no man taught* him the gospel he means particularly that no one taught him that Jews and Gentiles are equal. Although it seems that he was not in Jerusalem during the Passion and Crucifixion of Jesus, he was certainly there when Stephen was martyred. As a zealous Pharisee trying to root out this Christian heresy, he was bound to know what people like Stephen were claiming about Jesus: what he had said and done, and above all that God had raised him from the dead. Paul refers more than once to the contents of the gospel, which he was taught like other missionaries who had not been present in the Galilean and Jerusalem ministry of Jesus (e.g. 1 Cor. 15: 3). He obviously does not mean that the whole content of Christian doctrine was communicated to him at his conversion.

13. Paul's confession of his savage treatment of the Christians ties up with the account given in Acts of this period in his life. He seems to have played a prominent part in bringing about Stephen's death, and to have instigated the persecution that followed (Acts 7: 58 — 8: 3).

14. In his pre-Christian days Paul had dedicated his brilliant mind and boundless energy to studying, promoting and defending the Jewish faith as it had been handed down through the centuries. Elsewhere he tells us he was: 'circumcised on my eighth day, Israelite by race, of the tribe of Benjamin, a Hebrew born and bred; in my attitude to the law, a Pharisee; in pious zeal, a persecutor of the church; in legal rectitude, faultless' (Phil. 3: 5–6). It was as clear to Paul then as it was to Stephen—unlike the Twelve and the Jerusalem Christians generally—that Christianity and Judaism would not mix. As a zealous Pharisee, Paul was bound to try to stamp out a movement which challenged Israel's claim to be the People of God.

15–16. Then the incredible happened and the arch-persecutor became the devoted disciple. Read the accounts of Paul's conversion while he was on the road to Damascus to ferret out more Christians for punishment. It is narrated on three occasions (Acts 9: 1–9; 22: 5–11; 26: 12–18) and, like the account of Jesus' Baptism in the gospels, presumably it is based on a description of the experience recounted at a later date. The sudden conversion of a bigoted, cruel man into a great-hearted, selfless servant of Christ is a mystery that is ultimately beyond rational understanding. It was in Paul's case as unexpected for him as it is for us. Yet there are hints in the narrative of Acts and in Paul's letters that can help us to see how it came about.

AUGUSTINE'S VIEW

Augustine said that if Stephen had not prayed, the Church would not have had Paul. Undoubtedly the sight of a man undergoing martyrdom by stoning, with a prayer on his lips for forgiveness for his tormentors, must have done something to a rabbi who was after all schooled in the Old Testament teaching about a God of mercy and compassion. Could the Law be right if it sent to his death a man who, whatever his dangerous heresies might be, was clearly God-fearing, charitable and honourable?

If we may take Rom. 7 as Paul's own confession of how he had failed as a rabbi to find in the Law the way to peace of mind and to the presence of God, we may see another pointer towards his growing uneasiness about his position. This is surely what he means when he says: 'I should never have known what it was to covet, if the law had not said, "Thou shalt not covet"' (Rom. 7: 7). He must also have wondered whether the harrying of helpless people—Christians or anyone else—could be in accordance with the will of God. Paul was, after all, not a thug but a devoted son of the Old Testament faith, and it must have been increasingly impossible to square that with what he was doing. Is there a hint of all these doubts and uncertainties in some of the words Paul is reported to have heard Jesus say to him at his conversion: 'It is hard for you, this kicking against the goad' (Acts 26: 14), and is his redoubled fury against the Christians after Stephen's death the mark of a man trying to kill his growing suspicion that they might after all be right?

At all events the issue for Paul was plain. Jesus had been condemned and put to death for blasphemy, in accordance with the Law. In the light of the most sacred God-given truth which had been revealed to Israel uniquely among the nations, and to which Paul was heart and soul committed, Jesus was under the curse of God (3: 13). But if, as the Christians said, God had raised Jesus from the dead—and admittedly no one had been able to produce his dead body to refute this unthinkable claim—then God would have been revoking his own most holy Law and making it no longer absolute and infallible. Moreover, Jesus could not have been the Messiah, for the Pharisees maintained that when Israel as a nation lived in perfect obedience to the Law, Messiah would come, and not before. But the people were far from obeying the Law and even a devout Pharisee like Paul himself had found it impossible.

This was why the claims of the Christians were to the zealous Paul monstrous and preposterous. And this was why his sudden vision on the Damascus road of Jesus not as the crucified felon but as the Christ victorious over death struck him senseless and temporarily blinded him. We can only conjecture the tumult of mind, the shame and remorse, that seized Paul then and doubtless remained with him until the ministrations of Ananias and his baptism (Acts 9: 10–19) assured him of God's forgiveness and launched him into his new life as a Christian missionary.

As he looks back on that moment, here and elsewhere in his letters, it is to him nothing less than the death of the man he had been and the birth of the man he had now become. It was the turning point of his life. Now it seemed to him that God had destined him for this from his birth and had called him as he had called Jeremiah (Jer. 1: 5) and other prophets. No doubt it took time for Paul to work out the implications of his vision of the risen Christ, but all that he thought and did from then on was dependent on his conversion experience.

He was to preach a gospel of grace, since God had now made it plain that salvation does not depend on fulfilling the Law but on accepting God's gracious offer of new life in Christ. He was to preach Christ not as the Jewish Messiah, like the conservative Jerusalem Christians, but, as Stephen did, as the Saviour of the world. And he was to proclaim Christ as Son of God to the Gentiles, since the new relationship to Jesus which had made him henceforth a man 'in Christ' was available for all mankind and had nothing to do with Jewish ceremonial or ritual law.

17. Paul's experience had been so overpowering and so obviously God-given that he had had no urge to rush off to the Jerusalem apostles to seek confirmation of it or advice on what he should do. Indeed it would seem on the face of it that he had far more need of a spell of solitude and reflexion. This would appear to be the point of his mention of *Arabia*. The desert area around Damascus was included under this name, and it is much more likely that in the tradition of the

Old Testament prophets, and of Jesus himself after his Baptism, his vital concern was to be alone with his thoughts and to wrestle with his problem before God. Luke omits this in Acts, as is natural, and goes on to describe Paul's earliest activity as a Christian missionary in Damascus which Paul confirms here (Acts 9: 20–5). *

PAUL'S FIRST VISIT TO JERUSALEM

Three years later I did go up to Jerusalem to get to know 18 Cephas. I stayed with him for a fortnight, without seeing 19 any other of the apostles, except James the Lord's brother. What I write is plain truth; before God I am not lying. 20

Next I went to the regions of Syria and Cilicia, and 21, 22 remained unknown by sight to Christ's congregations in Judaea. They only heard it said, 'Our former persecutor 23 is preaching the good news of the faith which once he tried to destroy'; and they praised God for me. 24

* 18. *Three years later:* it is more likely that Paul dates events in his life from his conversion, his great turning-point, than from less important occasions. Here, for example, when he says 'three years later', he probably means three years after his conversion rather than three years after he came back to Damascus from Arabia. The dating of the events in Paul's life, including his conversion, is, however, quite difficult. Scholars have argued over the matter without reaching agreement. The best we can do in a commentary of this size is to suggest a series of dates which seems to fit in best with the various pieces of evidence and which is both reasonable and self-consistent.

The time-chart of the New Testament in the introductory volume to this series of commentaries, *Understanding the New Testament* (p. 53), would suggest later dates for Paul's conversion and the writing of this letter than those given in this commentary. Both viewpoints are possible. If we take A.D. 29 as the date of the Crucifixion, a good case can be made out for putting the conversion of Paul in A.D. 32. That would mean that Paul's first visit to Jerusalem referred to here took place in A.D. 35.

Cephas is the Aramaic form of Peter's name. Presumably he was called this by the ultra-Jewish propagandists who were questioning Paul's credentials. Paul is emphasizing the fact that it was not until three years after his conversion that he even made the acquaintance of Peter.

19. The apt comment has been made that presumably Paul and Peter did not spend the whole fortnight discussing the weather. It would be an obvious purpose of such a visit to put to Peter a whole variety of questions about what Jesus had said on this or that topic which had cropped up in the course of Paul's missionary work. Paul regarded himself as Peter's opposite number—the one as the apostle to the Jews and the other as the apostle to the Gentiles—but Peter had after all been the close companion of Jesus throughout his ministry.

Paul stresses the fact, however, that this was purely a private visit and not that of a second-rate apostle trying to get himself upgraded. He therefore insists that he met none of the rest of the Twelve at that time. In other words, if he is now being accused by the fanatical Judaizers who are upsetting the congregations in Galatia of perverting the gospel which he had been authorized to preach by the Twelve, he is making it quite plain that he never received any such commission from them. He never even saw them on the one occasion which would have been the obvious time for this to have happened.

James, the Lord's brother: it is not clear from the Greek whether Paul means that he regarded James as an 'apostle' or whether he simply means that he met Peter and, apart from him, only the man who later became the acknowledged head of the Jerusalem congregation. James (Mark 6: 3) may have been a full brother of Jesus, or a step-brother if Joseph was previously married, or, less likely, a cousin. He was no doubt sceptical of Jesus's Messiahship during his ministry (cf. Mark 3: 21, 31) but was presumably converted by his encounter with the risen Christ (1 Cor. 15: 7). Perhaps it was because of his relationship with Jesus that he became the head of the Jerusalem church. He was certainly the foremost supporter of the more exclusive Jewish Christian position. He is said to have been an extremely devout and orthodox Jew and for this reason he would be more acceptable to the Jewish religious leaders than the Twelve. The New Testament Letter of James may have been written by him.

The narrative of Acts 9: 26–30 dealing with this period in Paul's life describes the Jerusalem Christians as being still suspicious of Paul until Barnabas vouched for him. It speaks of Paul's having argued publicly in defence of Christianity, as a result of which his life was in danger, as it had been at Damascus, and it was thought best for him to leave the city. There is nothing in this which is inconsistent with Paul's own version here. The 'apostles' whom Paul met on this occasion (Acts 9: 27) were no doubt Peter and James.

21–4. Paul describes the next stage in his missionary career as having been spent in the area north of Palestine, in Syria and the adjacent territory of Cilicia. Luke's account locates his activities more precisely in Tarsus, chief city of Cilicia and Paul's own birthplace. This period, which lasted for several years, as we learn in 2: 1, is a closed book. We can only conjecture that it was in the course of these years that Paul's thought crystallized and his theology evolved as he faced the day-to-day problems of translating the Palestinian gospel into terms which would be understood by non-Jews. It may have been in this period that he encountered many of the hazards and hardships to which he refers in 2 Cor. 11: 24–7 and of which the book of Acts tells us so little. Paul's main concern here is to point out that all this time he had no contact with the Palestinian Christian congregations, apart from his fleeting visit to Jerusalem, but that they approved of all that they heard of his activities. ✫

2: 1–21   APOSTLE TO THE GENTILES

PAUL'S SECOND VISIT TO JERUSALEM

2 Next, fourteen years later, I went again to Jerusalem with
2 Barnabas, taking Titus with us. I went up because it had
been revealed by God that I should do so. I laid before
them—but at a private interview with the men of repute
—the gospel which I am accustomed to preach to the
Gentiles, to make sure that the race I had run, and was
3 running, should not be run in vain. Yet even my companion Titus, Greek though he is, was not compelled to
4 be circumcised. That course was urged only as a concession
to certain sham-Christians, interlopers who had stolen in
to spy upon the liberty we enjoy in the fellowship of
Christ Jesus. These men wanted to bring us into bondage,
5 but not for one moment did I yield to their dictation; I
was determined that the full truth of the Gospel should
be maintained for you.

✳ 1. *fourteen years later*—than what?—than his first visit to
Jerusalem? More likely Paul means fourteen years after his
conversion, and his point is that in all that time he had only
two fleeting contacts with the recognized leaders of the Church
at Jerusalem. He could hardly therefore be described as having
been working as a missionary under their orders or with
their authorization. This second visit to Jerusalem would
bring us to the year A.D. 46. Meantime, as we have seen,
Paul had been busily engaged in missionary work in Syria
and Cilicia, and in particular at Tarsus, his native city.

But events had summoned him to play a larger role. As we
are told in Acts 11: 19 ff., the Christians who were driven
out of Jerusalem after Stephen's martyrdom had settled in
various parts of the Near East. Wherever they went they
took the gospel with them, and the persecution which was

designed to suppress the Christian heresy served only to make it more widespread. Foremost among these new centres of Christian mission was the city of Antioch, the capital of the province of Syria, a cosmopolitan place with a population of half a million. Here, as a result of Christian missionary work, a thriving congregation was growing up including many Gentiles. It was at Antioch that the followers of the Way, or the Nazarenes, as they had been called, now came to be known as Christians, and the word which was probably first used as a nickname—like Methodists and Quakers—became a title which they bore with pride. The conservative Jerusalem church, perturbed at a development which in their view might affect the historical Jewish character of the Faith, sent Barnabas to Antioch to investigate.

BARNABAS FETCHES PAUL TO ANTIOCH

He, good man that he was, realized very quickly that God was powerfully at work in Antioch and that what was needed was a leader who was familiar with the Gentile outlook and who had worked among pagans before. And for this assignment who could be better than Paul? So off goes Barnabas to Tarsus to find him, brings him back to Antioch, and for a year they work together building up a sizable congregation.

Some time before this, a Christian prophet from Jerusalem, by name Agabus, had visited Antioch and had predicted a severe and widespread famine. When this started in A.D. 46, the Christians at Antioch, as a token of their solidarity with the mother-church at Jerusalem and also as an act of compassion, made a collection among themselves and sent their gift, either in cash or kind, to Jerusalem in the care of Paul and Barnabas. This, then, is the visit which Paul now describes in his letter to the Galatians, although it is not the handing over of the gift to the leaders of the Jerusalem church which is at this point uppermost in Paul's mind.

FAMINE RELIEF AND OTHER MATTERS

Barnabas had been sent to investigate the situation of the Gentile mission at Antioch. According to Acts, this is the first time he has had an opportunity to make a report on it to the Jerusalem church authorities. It was therefore natural that the whole question of the conditions under which Gentiles should be admitted to the Church should come up for discussion and that Paul should put forward his own point of view and defend his practice. A third member of the party, Titus, who is not mentioned by Luke in Acts, is referred to here in such a way as to suggest that he would not have been mentioned by Paul either if he had not become the centre of a storm which is described in the following verses.

2. Paul makes it quite plain, however, that he was not summoned to Jerusalem by the apostles to account for his actions. He regarded his visit as having taken place because *it had been revealed by God* that he should go to Jerusalem, no doubt a reference to the inspired prophecy of Agabus which had prompted the collection for the famine-stricken mother-church.

What Paul describes is *a private interview*, not a public meeting or a court of the Church. Those present he refers to as *the men of repute*, or later in verse 9 as *those reputed pillars of our society*, where he identifies them as James (the Lord's brother), Cephas (Peter), and John (the son of Zebedee). Although there is nothing disparaging about the apostles in Paul's description, it is difficult not to feel that a note of resentment has crept in, understandable enough if his opponents, as is likely, used these phrases to contrast the authority of the Jerusalem apostles with his own. The topic which they discussed was not only Paul's passionately held conviction that Gentiles must be admitted into the Church without being obliged to conform to Jewish Law, but his general presentation of the Faith.

Let us not forget that for the greatest part of the fourteen years since his conversion Paul had been on his own. He had had to work out his own interpretation of the gospel in the light of his conversion experience and such guidance as he had received from other missionaries in his early days as a Christian. He had also had to evolve his own missionary technique in dealing with largely Gentile communities. If he now found that what he had been saying and doing did not meet with the approval of the leading Jewish Christians, he would no doubt carry on as before, but it would have meant that there were two Christian Churches, not one, which to Paul would have been a contradiction in terms. To that extent his work among the Gentiles, with its insistence that there was but one Church, open to Jews and Gentiles on equal terms, would have been *in vain*.

THE CASE OF TITUS

3–5. But this, he goes on, is precisely what did not happen. Far from challenging his interpretation of the gospel, the apostles were in full agreement with it. They even accepted the presence of Titus, an uncircumcised Gentile Christian, there in the centre of Jewish Christianity, despite the opposition of some fanatical upholders of the thesis that all Christians must submit to this Jewish rite. Paul does not mince his words as he trounces these *sham-Christians* and their underhand methods. For Paul to yield on this point would have been to make nonsense of his whole missionary effort.

The case of Titus was obviously a major issue, garbled details of which had reached the Galatians. Yet, if we look again at Paul's words here, the sense is distinctly ambiguous. Some commentators would therefore maintain that Paul had a guilty conscience about this particular occasion, that Titus was circumcised, as a sop to Jewish-Christian feelings, and that the most Paul can now say is that he permitted it as a special concession within the Holy City while opposing it in principle. It could be argued that on a later occasion he sacrificed principle to expediency in the case of the circumcision of Timothy (Acts 16: 3). But Timothy was half-Jewish, and Paul never suggested that Jewish Christians should not observe the time-honoured requirements of national tradition.

He is obviously unhappy about the whole incident, and it may well be that under pressure he had agreed to some kind of concession to Jewish-Christian feelings about the presence of an uncircumcised Gentile in their midst, perhaps a temporary segregation of Titus which Paul afterwards regretted. But to agree to his circumcision even in these highly special circumstances would surely have been to cut the ground from under his own feet, to give away his whole case, and to undermine the impression which he is laboriously trying to create, namely that the leaders of the Church supported his views and policy up to the hilt. If it had come to an issue, Paul as we know him would more probably have preferred to send Titus back to Antioch, and if the worst had come to the worst, to have gone back himself with him, without the blessing of the apostles which he now goes on to describe.✳

PAUL AND BARNABAS ARE APPROVED

6 But as for the men of high reputation (not that their importance matters to me: God does not recognize these personal distinctions)—these men of repute, I say, did not
7 prolong the consultation, but on the contrary acknowledged that I had been entrusted with the Gospel for Gentiles as surely as Peter had been entrusted with the
8 Gospel for Jews. For God whose action made Peter an apostle to the Jews, also made me an apostle to the Gentiles.

9   Recognizing, then, the favour thus bestowed upon me, those reputed pillars of our society, James, Cephas, and John, accepted Barnabas and myself as partners, and shook

hands upon it, agreeing that we should go to the Gentiles while they went to the Jews. All they asked was that we 10 should keep their poor in mind, which was the very thing I made it my business to do.

* 6–8. The *importance* of the Twelve, and for that matter of James also, in the eyes of Paul's opponents was that they had, unlike him, been associated with Jesus during his lifetime. But for Paul this is of no more significance than the fact of his own summons by the risen Christ to be an apostle. Nevertheless, the point that matters is that three of the acknowledged leaders of the Church were completely satisfied with Paul's account of his activities. They recognized that God had called Paul to a special sphere of service among the Gentiles as surely as he had given Peter oversight of the mission to the Jews.

9–10. Paul now concludes his account of his second visit to Jerusalem by saying that far from having been put in his place, or receiving an apostolic commission, two of the foremost of the Twelve and the acknowledged head of the Jewish-Christian mother-church, having heard Paul's story, accepted Barnabas and himself as *partners* in the common task of proclaiming the same gospel. Giving them the right hand of fellowship they agreed that while they themselves would concentrate mainly on Palestine, Paul and Barnabas would spread the faith in the foreign field. Finally—and Paul mentions it almost as an anti-climax—the only direct request of the Church leaders was that Paul and Barnabas should bear in mind the hardships of the relatively poor Jerusalem church, which was precisely what had brought them to Jerusalem in the first place!

DOES ACTS SQUARE WITH GALATIANS?

We have been assuming throughout the narrative that this second visit of Paul to Jerusalem is to be identified with the famine-relief visit described in Acts 11. Some scholars, however, take the view that what Paul has just been describing is what Luke records in Acts 15, and that this is therefore Paul's version of the Council of Jerusalem. But what Paul describes here is a private interview. What Acts 15 describes is a public meeting. Has Luke invented the Council and its decrees or has he made two visits out of one? In either case the reliability of Acts is called in question.

To avoid that conclusion it is suggested that Paul might have overlooked the 'famine visit'. This would be quite extraordinary, since he is at the greatest pains to point out that he is writing here nothing but the 'plain truth' (1: 20) about his contacts with the Jerusalem church. It seems to present fewest difficulties if we give Paul credit for being truthful, treat Luke's narrative as basically accurate, and regard the Council of Jerusalem described in Acts 15 as having taken place during Paul's *third* visit to the Holy City, that is, after this letter was written (see p. 13). ✳

PAUL VERSUS PETER

11 But when Cephas came to Antioch, I opposed him to his
12 face, because he was clearly in the wrong. For until certain persons came from James he was taking his meals with gentile Christians, but when they came he drew back and began to hold aloof, because he was afraid
13 of the advocates of circumcision. The other Jewish Christians showed the same lack of principle; even Barnabas was carried away and played false like the rest.
14 But when I saw that their conduct did not square with the truth of the Gospel, I said to Cephas, before the whole congregation, 'If you, a Jew born and bred, live like a Gentile, and not like a Jew, how can you insist that Gentiles must live like Jews?'

✻ 11. Paul now goes on to refer to an incident which, he would claim, showed how little he was under the thumb of the apostles. This was an occasion when he actually took Peter, the chief apostle, to task in a public assembly and accused him of being two-faced in his attitude to the message of the gospel.

He does not specify when this battle of words took place, but it would seem most likely that it was after Paul had returned from his second visit to Jerusalem to his headquarters at Antioch, and before he set out on his first missionary journey, in the course of which he founded the churches in Galatia to which he is writing this letter. This ties up very well with Luke's narrative in Acts, where we are told how Paul and Barnabas returned to Antioch from their famine-relief visit to Jerusalem, bringing John Mark, the author of the second gospel, with them (Acts 12: 25); how they set out from there under divine prompting on a missionary tour to Cyprus and Asia Minor, including Galatia (Acts 13, 14), only to find on their return to Antioch that the congregation there was being split in two by some of the narrow Jewish-Christian advocates of circumcision as essential for all Christians, including Gentiles (Acts 15: 1–2).

It was this type of propaganda which made the Council of Jerusalem necessary, and, as we have seen (p. 11), it was the same propaganda by the same type of people which was now upsetting the Galatian churches and which called forth this letter. Jewish-Christian extremists, claiming that all Christians must conform with the full requirements of Mosaic Law, were repudiated at the Council of Jerusalem even by James, the leader of the Jewish Christians, and certainly had no support from Peter, who had been convinced once and for all by the events associated with the conversion of Cornelius (Acts 10) that God meant the Church to be open to Jews and Gentiles alike by acceptance of Christ as Saviour and by baptism.

TABLE-FELLOWSHIP

✶ 12–13. What Paul accuses Peter of here, however, is a milder form of the same dangerous heresy as was being propagated by the extremists. Peter on a visit to the Antioch community had been quite happy to associate freely with the Gentile Christians. This involved having meals in common. Although eating with Gentiles was not specifically forbidden by the Law of Moses, it had become traditional practice among orthodox Jews, in order to avoid any risk of eating 'unclean' food or of being contaminated by using utensils which had been in contact with it, that Jews and Gentiles should not sit down at the same table.

Peter, who shared Paul's view that this sort of thing had no more to do with salvation than circumcision had, on this occasion had nevertheless had an attack of cold feet. Some of these extremists came down from Jerusalem to Antioch, not necessarily sent by James, but obviously sharing his viewpoint. We are told specifically that such people acted without instructions from the Jerusalem church and were disowned by it (Acts 15: 24). But their presence was enough to make Peter have qualms about his own attitude.

Was he right, he must have wondered, to throw overboard the tradition in which he had been brought up? Admittedly these Gentile Christians were his brothers in Christ, baptized into the same Church, acknowledging the same Saviour. But was he not as a Jew bound to respect the legacy of history? Might he not be sacrificing a precious principle? Barnabas and the rest of the Jewish Christians shared his misgivings and followed his example in withdrawing from the common table. Whether they went off by themselves to another room or another house we are not told. At all events complete fellowship was for the time being at an end.

14. For Paul, however, this was a sheer betrayal of the gospel. It struck at the very roots of what it meant to be a Christian. Whatever principle Peter thought he was respect-

ing was of no significance compared with the gospel principle that he was violating. And since this was a public issue that affected the life of the congregation, it was not something that could be smoothed over or dealt with by a quiet word with Peter in private. Paul could not have challenged Peter openly as he did had he not been sure that basically Peter and he were of one heart and mind on the matter. What he was objecting to was Peter's temporary agreement for reasons of expediency with a policy in which neither he nor Paul believed.

WHAT WAS AT STAKE?

Peter, when he came to Antioch, had rightly recognized that a Jewish Christian is a Christian first and a Jew second. What he had now done in a moment of weakness would make a divided Church inevitable or a united Church impossible. What Paul says to him here, obviously quoting the scornful accusation of the extremists, is that he who was quite ready to *live like a Gentile* (by disregarding Jewish restrictions) was now forcing the Gentiles to the point that if they wanted to remain Christians they would have to become Jews.

Paul's logic was irresistible. It may have seemed a small point that Peter should on grounds of expediency temporarily give countenance to the supporters of Jewish traditionalism. But in effect he was paving the way for the death of the Church. For the chief apostle to yield to the extremists on this point would end in their demanding of the Gentile Christians total acceptance of the Mosaic Law, including circumcision. Since most Gentiles would refuse to comply, this would mean either two parallel Churches or, more likely, the end of the Gentile mission. Christianity would then become a Jewish sect with a doubtful future. Paul sized up the situation with the same unerring instinct as he was later to show in his appreciation of the Christian attitude to slavery in his letter to Philemon. There, without questioning the practice of slavery, he made it inevitable that ultimately

41

Christians could no longer tolerate it. Here without disputing the validity of certain particular religious traditions he makes it impossible for Christians ultimately to regard them as absolute. *

JUSTIFICATION BY FAITH

15 We ourselves are Jews by birth, not Gentiles and sinners.
16 But we know that no man is ever justified by doing what the law demands, but only through faith in Christ Jesus; so we too have put our faith in Jesus Christ, in order that we might be justified through this faith, and not through deeds dictated by law; for by such deeds, Scripture says, no mortal man shall be justified.

17 If now, in seeking to be justified in Christ, we ourselves no less than the Gentiles turn out to be sinners against the
18 law, does that mean that Christ is an abettor of sin? No, never! No, if I start building up again a system which I have pulled down, then it is that I show myself up as a
19 transgressor of the law. For through the law I died to
20 law—to live for God. I have been crucified with Christ: the life I now live is not my life, but the life which Christ lives in me; and my present bodily life is lived by faith in the Son of God, who loved me and sacrificed himself
21 for me. I will not nullify the grace of God; if righteousness comes by law, then Christ died for nothing.

* 15. Paul begins by identifying himself with Peter. Both of them are *Jews by birth*, members of the community with which God had established a special relationship, and *not Gentiles and sinners*. Paul probably meant these last words to be in inverted commas, since 'Gentiles = sinners' was the normal equation that would be made by the Jewish-Christian extremists. For them anyone who did not comply with the

God-given Law of Moses was bound to be a sinner, whether he was a Jew or a Gentile. One of the charges that the Pharisees had made against Jesus was that he had consorted with 'publicans and sinners'—tax-collectors in the employment of the Roman government and the less respectable members of society.

But in a sense all Jews were entitled to equate the Gentile world with a sinful world. Paul himself in his letters to the churches at Rome and Corinth recognized the gulf that existed between the general moral tone of any Jewish community and any Gentile community, despite the virtues of many Gentiles and the lapses of many Jews. It was not only nationalistic fervour or self-righteous pride that entitled the Jews to call themselves the 'chosen people'. Their standards of behaviour were undoubtedly considerably higher than those of the pagans.

16. As Paul goes on, however, Peter and the particular incident at Antioch are forgotten, and as he writes these words to the Galatians he is much more proclaiming his deepest convictions about the meaning of the Christian faith than dealing with a particular issue. The same thing happens in his letter to the Philippians, where, having started by mentioning a storm in a teacup between two women in the congregation at Philippi, his mind soars upward from this minor squabble and gives birth to one of his greatest pronouncements (Phil. 4: 2-9).

So here he is speaking not only for Peter and himself but for all believers as he asserts the cardinal Christian principle of 'justification by faith'. Paul uses many words which are no longer everyday currency in the twentieth century—redemption, salvation, sanctification among others—but none has been subject to so much misunderstanding as justification. We are sometimes told that this word and what it stands for is the key to Paul's theology. At other times we are told that it is merely one metaphor among many which the apostle uses to convey his ideas. It would be most unlikely that a mind as fertile as Paul's, which in his letters was constantly throwing out new lines of thought, flying off at a tangent, sometimes almost incoherent, could be tied down to any one way of expressing the essence of his understanding of Christianity. Paul was not a writer of textbooks but a creative artist and something of a poet. Moreover, when this particular idea is adopted by some types of Protestantism as a bulwark against Rome, one is entitled to suspect that Paul is being used for purposes of which he would not have approved.

We are on surer ground if we think of justification by faith as being one of the most deeply rooted convictions in the mind of the apostle, which he expounds at length in this letter and at greater length in the letter to the Romans. It is true that 'justification' is a metaphor from the law courts, but it is much more a question of how we can get into the right relationship with God. A judge 'justifies' a prisoner when he treats him as innocent although he knows he is guilty. This makes nonsense in law but, says Paul, this is exactly how God treats us.

We are all without any doubt sinners. There is a gulf between us and God. How can we bridge that gulf? Not, says Paul, by trying to acquire merit in the sight of God by doing good (or in the case of the Jews, by striving to comply with all the provisions of the Law of Moses) but by committing our lives wholly to Christ. When we do that, God accepts us as we are, forgives our sins and begins to transform us into his sons and daughters as we were meant to be. Although we still remain sinners, God treats us as though we are not guilty. No efforts of our own can accomplish this, it is an act of God's sheer love. Paul presses home his point by quoting Ps. 143: 2, *no mortal man shall be justified* (verse 16), adding his own comment, *by such deeds.*

17–18. Well then, he says, if we Jews recognize now as Christians that we are just as great sinners as the Gentiles, does that mean that it is Christ who has made us sinners? What nonsense! The exact opposite is true. We have recognized that it is only through faith in Christ and not through trying to comply with the demands of the Law that we can get right with God. If we then start to bring obedience to the Law back into our lives we really are admitting that we have been guilty of a serious crime in ever accepting Christ as our only Saviour. We are implying that we should have done better to rely on compliance with the Law to save us as we were brought up to do.

BACK TO THE DAMASCUS ROAD

19. Then Paul turns to his own experience. It was through his failure to live up to the standard that the Law demanded, through his recognition that the best that the Law could do was to show him what a sinner he was, that he learned how inadequate a means it was to make men at one with God. He tells us how he wrestled with this problem in Rom. 7: 7 ff. It was not the fault of the Law that he could not live up to it. The fault lay in himself. 'The good which I want to do, I fail to do' (Rom. 7: 19). But now he had seen that the real value of the Law had been to lead him to the point where he committed himself to Christ, who alone could enable him to *live for God*. For him now the Law was a dead letter.

20. So he comes back, as he always must, to the great moment on the Damascus road when Christ called him and he responded. This was far from the end of his spiritual pilgrimage, but it was the end of his despair. The old Paul died—not only the cruel little persecutor of the Christians, hating himself for it as we may surmise, but also the virtuous Pharisee who knew that his virtue was a hollow pretence, the godly rabbi who knew that his inner life was a travesty of what he professed in public. So he can say, *I have been crucified with Christ*. In his own experience he has died to the past and risen to a new life. And like every Christian in the early Church he had symbolized it in his baptism by immersion, going down into the water, washing away his evil past, and rising from the water cleansed, to face a no less difficult

future, but with inner peace and the certainty that Christ was with him.

So, contrasting the bigoted persecutor that he once had been with the courageous ambassador for Christ that he had now become, Paul is compelled to say *the life I now live is not my life*. How could it be? Something, some One, had come into his life, and whatever good he was able to do was done because Christ lived in him.

Life for him was now lived in a new dimension. He had given his allegiance to Christ, not as to a revered teacher or even as to the Messiah but as to the Son of God. He had done this because of what Christ had done for him. Christ *loved me and sacrificed himself for me*. Paul had known Jesus in his earthly ministry no more than we have. Yet, if there is any point in this letter where he speaks directly to us today, it is here. This is the heart of the matter. King, Messiah, Lord—yes, all that, but basically what brings us to our knees is this echo of Jesus' own words: 'There is no greater love than this, that a man should lay down his life for his friends' (John 15: 13).

21. So Paul concludes, as he must, by acknowledging what is to us, as to him, the supreme miracle, that God should have shown his love for man so marvellously and movingly on Calvary. Compared with this, the trivial requirements of the Law as a means of getting right with God were clearly futile. Christianity is a religion of *grace*, that is, of God's determination that despite our folly he will make us what he meant us to be. We cannot do this by ourselves. Only God can enable us to do it, and this he has done by sending his Son, 'that everyone who has faith in him may not die but have eternal life' (John 3: 16). Indeed, says Paul, if we could come into the right relationship with God by our own unaided efforts there need never have been a cross on Calvary. *

3: 1-29: FAITH OR LAW

PAUL APPEALS TO EXPERIENCE

You stupid Galatians! You must have been bewitched— **3** you before whose eyes Jesus Christ was openly displayed upon his cross! Answer me one question: did you re- **2** ceive the Spirit by keeping the law or by believing the gospel message? Can it be that you are so stupid? You **3** started with the spiritual; do you now look to the material to make you perfect? Have all your great ex- **4** periences been in vain—if vain indeed they should be? I ask **5** then: when God gives you the Spirit and works miracles among you, why is this? Is it because you keep the law, or is it because you have faith in the gospel message?

✴ 1. Paul has been carried by the intensity of his feelings far from the incident at Antioch (2: 11) that started off this train of thought. It has led him to give a moving and personal testimony to what the Gospel has meant for him (2: 20). He has been so stirred that now, as he recalls the unmistakable evidence of the living power of Christ in the recent campaign among the Galatians, and reflects that these same people are now prepared to listen to agitators who tell them that what really matters is being circumcised and obeying the Law of Moses, he bursts out in affectionate exasperation: You crazy people! You must be out of your minds!

He tells them they *must have been bewitched*, somebody must have put a spell on them. They knew all about black magic in pagan cities like Iconium and the other towns of the Galatian mission. Sorcerers and spell-binders were plentiful. These Jewish-Christian extremists must have hypnotized you, says Paul wryly. If you had kept your eyes fixed on the Cross of Christ and all that it means, he adds, you would never have fallen for this rubbish.

2. He urges them to think back to the time when Barnabas and he first proclaimed the gospel message among them. What had happened then, as happened everywhere in these early days of the Church, as we can read in the book of Acts, was that ordinary men and women, who were moved by the preaching of the missionaries to break with the past and begin a new life through accepting Christ as their Lord and Saviour, found themselves uplifted and exhilarated by a new sense of freedom, peace and joy. Did any of that, asks Paul bluntly, have the slightest thing to do with observing the terms of the Law?

3. This appeal to the personal experience of the Galatians is rammed home by Paul's next words. What made them Christians was the grace of God—a *spiritual* thing. What changed their lives was the power of God's Spirit. But now they are prepared to listen to men who say that purely *material* things, like circumcision and a regulated diet, are of the very essence of Christianity. Without them, they say, no one can be a good Christian.

4. Can it be, continues the apostle, that all that the Galatians themselves have experienced of the new quality of life—with its stresses and strains as much as its exhilarations and enthusiasms—can all this have made no lasting impact upon them? He can hardly credit it.

5. They feel that they are living in a new dimension, where things happen that could not ordinarily happen, such as changed lives, the healing of the sick, the restoration to sanity of the mentally unbalanced. Do they attribute this to a meticulous observance of the Law of Moses or to their venture of faith in the power of the living Christ which first made them members of his Body, the Church? In the narrative of the mission of Paul and Barnabas to Galatia in Acts 13–14, specific mention is made of the cure of a cripple at Lystra (Acts 14: 8–10) but general reference is also made to 'signs and miracles' which the missionaries performed at Iconium (14: 3). No doubt this had been typical of the whole campaign.

Paul's appeal in these verses has been to recent converts from paganism. To judge its effectiveness we have to remember three factors which differentiated the early Church from the Church today. One was that unless they had been Jews or 'God-fearers' (see p. 7), converts to Christianity living in pagan cities literally stepped into a new life—from meaningless idol-worship to the knowledge of a loving God; from a world in the grip of blind fate or the stars into a world which had meaning and purpose; from a society where for many people moral standards meant little to a community where compassion, charity and integrity had pride of place. The contrast between the old and the new life was therefore much greater than that which is experienced by people today who become confirmed Christians after having been brought up in Christian homes, or having lived in countries which are nominally Christian.

A second difference was that in the early Church, from Pentecost onwards, the presence of the Holy Spirit was almost visible. Converts were caught up into an infectious religious ecstasy such as was known in the early days of prophecy in Old Testament times, and which has since been seen in the history of the Church in periods of religious revival. It is still found in some Christian communities today. Paul recognized the value of this as evidence of the presence of the Spirit, but had to issue a cautionary warning that it should not get out of hand or be regarded as the most important gift that the Spirit could bestow (1 Cor. 12–14).

Thirdly, there was the fact that in these early days the apostles, using the word in the widest sense, had the power to heal the sick. Our problem today is not to account for that, since Jesus had promised that those who believed in him would share his healing power (John 14: 12), but to ask why the Church as a whole no longer has it. Part of the answer was given by Jesus himself to his disciples when they were unable to cure an epileptic boy. He told them that healing came through prayer (Mark 9: 14 ff.). Part of the answer lies in the development of medical science and a different understanding of what diseases are. Perhaps in the little intercessory groups for divine healing that meet in various branches of the Church today, we may see the beginning of a breakthrough at a time when we are becoming more and more conscious of the unity of mind and body, spirit and matter. *

PAUL APPEALS TO SCRIPTURE

6 Look at Abraham: he put his faith in God, and that faith was counted to him as righteousness.

7 You may take it, then, that it is the men of faith who
8 are Abraham's sons. And Scripture, foreseeing that God would justify the Gentiles through faith, declared the Gospel to Abraham beforehand: 'In you all nations shall
9 find blessing.' Thus it is the men of faith who share the blessing with faithful Abraham.

* 6. Having challenged the Galatians to say whether all these evidences of the work of the Spirit among them were to be attributed ultimately to their observance of the Law of Moses or ultimately to the fact that they had committed themselves by an act of faith to Christ, Paul now confronts them with the evidence of Scripture, which was, of course, accepted as the Word of God equally by Gentile Christians and Jewish Christians, by Paul as much as by the extremists.

We shall hear a good deal about Abraham in this chapter and the one following, and Paul has chosen to build his case on him with good reason. The Jews regarded Abraham as the ᴠ father of the race, singled out by God to be the foundation of God's special covenant relationship with Israel, to inherit the ᴠ Holy Land and to be the progenitor of many nations. All of this was sealed by the token of circumcision, the outward sign in Abraham and his descendants of their inward commitment to God (Gen. 17). Jews were by birth and circumcision automatically members of the People of God. Gentiles could, by circumcision and acceptance of the terms of the covenant as laid down in the Law, likewise become sons of Abraham.

Paul, however, like the author of the letter to the Hebrews, finds in the Scriptures a different, and for him a far more significant, reason for Abraham's place in history as the founder-member of the People of God. This had nothing to do with circumcision but everything to do with faith. He refers here to Gen. 15: 5–6 where Abraham received a promise from God that he would be the father of descendants as numerous as the stars in the sky. He had faith in this promise, and because of that God accepted him as a fit person to be the foundation stone of his plan for the salvation of the world through Israel. The author of the letter to the Hebrews is saying the same thing in a different way when he extols Abraham as a man whose life was built on faith. He went out into the unknown from Haran trusting only in God, not knowing where he was going, knowing only that God had called him to a great adventure (Heb. 11: 8–10).

7–9. So, says Paul, the real sons of Abraham are not those who belong to his nation but those who share his faith, those who have the same trusting acceptance of God's promises. Once again Paul quotes Genesis, this time Gen. 12: 3, where God pledges that in Abraham *all nations shall find blessing.* Now says Paul, very properly, what is the real meaning of this promise? Surely it is this, that God from the beginning planned to create and mould a community which would be the People of God, his instrument for the renewal of the life of the world.

Israel was intended to fulfil this role, but Israel failed. God has therefore reconstituted Israel into the new Israel, the Church, and now we can see how the old Israel's failure to be 'a light to the nations' (Isa. 42: 6) has been redressed by Christ and his Church. So the promise to Abraham has now been fulfilled in a deeper sense than even Abraham knew. He was being told the good news that God would welcome into the historic community of Israel all men of every race who were ready, like Abraham, to commit their lives to him. Thus, concludes Paul, those blessings which you have now received—the new life in the Spirit, the evidence of God's powerful acts among you—these are in fact the beginning of the fulfilment of the promise made so long ago to Abraham, who is thus, as he says elsewhere (Rom. 4: 16) 'the father of us all', father of the faithful, whether Jews or Gentiles. ✶

THE CURSE OF THE LAW

10 On the other hand those who rely on obedience to the law are under a curse; for Scripture says, 'Cursed are all who do not persevere in doing everything that is written
11 in the Book of the Law.' It is evident that no one is ever justified before God in terms of law; because we read,
12 'he shall gain life who is justified through faith'. Now law is not at all a matter of having faith: we read, 'he who does this shall gain life by what he does'.

13   Christ bought us freedom from the curse of the law by becoming for our sake an accursed thing; for Scripture
14 says, 'Cursed is everyone who is hanged on a tree.' And the purpose of it all was that the blessing of Abraham should in Jesus Christ be extended to the Gentiles, so that we might receive the promised Spirit through faith.

✶ 10. Now the apostle carries the attack into the enemy's camp. Not only does Scripture show, he says, that the true children of Abraham become such by faith and not by circumcision, which therefore means that Gentiles are included, but Scripture also shows that those who rely on the Law to save them do not receive the blessing of God but his *curse*. According to Deut. 27: 26, any Jew who does not fulfil the letter of the Law is accursed. Paul's own view was that that included everyone, since one of his most strongly held convictions was that all men are sinners. He expounds this view at length in his letter to the Romans (e.g. 3: 23) but he does not wish to do so here, since he is relying on Scripture to argue his case.

11. He turns next therefore to Habakkuk 2: 4 to demonstrate that obeying the Law can never bring a man into the right relationship with God: *he shall gain life who is justified through faith*. Habakkuk had used the word *faith* in the sense of 'faithfulness', meaning that what matters is that men should persevere through all difficulties in trustful reliance on God. Paul is thinking of *faith* in the sense of pledging our lives to Christ; but basically it comes to the same thing. His point is that the right relationship with God involves a personal act of allegiance and is not merely a matter of striving to live up to the demands of the Law. He also claims that the Old Testament shows that this is so.

Paul need not have resorted to one particular text to prove his case. The prevalent impression we get from the Old Testament, as for example in the Psalms, is that the Jews found the Law not a burden but a joy: that man is blessed who delights in the law of the Lord (Ps. 1: 2); 'the law is light' (Prov. 6: 23). The Pharisees in Paul's day had, however, made the Law a stranglehold on life, a deadweight of punctilious requirements which ordinary people did not attempt to cope with and which even the most conscientious Pharisees, like Paul himself, were unable to fulfil. It is this wrong attitude to the Law which Paul is attacking. But since he is dealing with people who argue along legal lines, he has to use the same kind of legalistic approach that his opponents resort to. In other words his real case does not depend on quoting texts, as he does here; but he has to meet these extremists on their own ground.

12. The Old Testament prophets and psalmists would have said that there is no opposition between complying with

the Law of Moses, properly understood, and having faith in God. These were two sides of the same coin. They would, however, have agreed with Paul that when the Law was turned into a fetish, as it was in his day by the Pharisees and these extremists who were in effect Christian Pharisees, obeying the Law and having faith *had* become two different things. So when Paul goes on to quote Lev. 18: 5, which says that if a man keeps the statutes of the Law he *shall gain life by what he does*, he can argue legitimately that, as the Law was understood by the rigorists, unless a man complied with its provisions to the last detail he would not *gain life* but death.

13. But, he goes on, if we are doomed to be forever estranged from God unless we observe the Law in every detail—an impossible assignment in any case, he would add, although on this point his opponents would not have agreed with him—we can only escape this fate by relying on what Christ has done on our behalf. It is quite clear from the Law that anyone who is executed as a criminal is doomed; the curse of God is upon him (Deut. 21: 23). But Christ voluntarily died such a death, he was *hanged on a tree*.

Jesus therefore broke the Law in the most violent way and technically became subject to the curse of God. Jewish Pharisees would say that this was true, but any Christian— and the extremists, whatever mistaken ideas they had, agreed with Paul that Christ was the Messiah and not a criminal— was bound to say that the Cross pointed to Christ's triumph and not to his failure. By transforming what was the death of an evil-doer, according to the Law, into the life of the Risen Messiah, the Resurrection had shown up the Law in its true colours.

The curse which the Law imposed on all who broke it was therefore rendered null and void by Christ. By identifying himself with us, he had taken the curse upon himself, put himself in our place, accepted the penalty that we deserved, so that we, by becoming incorporated in him through faith, are no longer liable to suffer the consequences of our failure.

In modern terms Paul might have said something like this: We are all sinners and could expect nothing but permanent separation from God, had it not been that Christ took on himself the punishment that we deserved, thus making us free to enter into a new relationship with God by trying to live as children of God in union with Christ.

14. So through Christ the promise made by God to Abraham has at last come true. The promise was that all nations should find blessing through the founding father of the People of God. For centuries the blessing had been limited to one nation, the Jews, and the few Gentiles who were prepared to become Jews by accepting the terms of the Law. But now that Christ had shown that the Law was an artificial barricade which wrongfully kept the Gentiles away from God, the way was open for men and women of all nations to receive the promised blessing through accepting Jesus as Lord of their lives. When they did so, the blessing, i.e. the power of the Spirit, came upon them and among them, as everybody involved in the Gentile mission had seen with his own eyes. ✻

PAUL APPEALS TO REASON

My brothers, let me give you an illustration. Even in 15 ordinary life, when a man's will and testament has been duly executed, no one else can set it aside or add a codicil. Now the promises were pronounced to Abraham and to 16 his 'issue'. It does not say 'issues' in the plural, but in the singular, 'and to your issue'; and the 'issue' intended is Christ. What I am saying is this: a testament, or covenant, 17 had already been validated by God; it cannot be invalidated, and its promises rendered ineffective, by a law made four hundred and thirty years later. If the inheritance is 18 by legal right, then it is not by promise; but it was by promise that God bestowed it as a free gift on Abraham.

✼ 15. Paul has argued for the primacy of faith over law from experience and Scripture. He now states the case from the angle of human reason. It is clear, he says, that if a man makes a will, only he and nobody else can alter it in any way. He is going on to say that in a sense the same thing was true of God's promise to Abraham. Having made it, only God himself could annul it, and certainly it could not be cancelled by the promulgation of the Law several centuries later. And the Law in addition, was given, not like the promise directly by God, but indirectly through angels (verse 19).

16. Then as if in parenthesis Paul makes a point which is much more than the grammatical quibble which on the surface it appears to be. It turns on the exact words of the promises made by God to Abraham in such passages as Gen. 13: 15 and 17: 7. Paul notes that the promises were made to Abraham and *to his issue*, singular and not plural; therefore it did not mean the descendants of Abraham as a whole but *the* descendant *par excellence*, namely the Messiah.

This may seem to us to be curious and far-fetched reasoning, more appropriate to the scholastic disputations which had been part of Paul's early training as a rabbi. But, after all, it was people with that type of mind who were upsetting the Galatian converts and who had to be fought with their own weapons. Moreover, Paul is, despite his reliance on a trifling point of grammar, expressing a deeply held conviction in the early Church, namely that, since in the Old Testament the coming Messiah was always regarded in some sense as a representative figure, incorporating the whole people, Christ must now be seen as fulfilling this role.

So Paul, like the author of Hebrews, thinks of Christ not only as pre-existent but also as being present throughout the history of Israel (e.g. 1 Cor. 10: 4; Heb. 11: 25-6), identifying himself with the fortunes and misfortunes of the People of God, and eventually by his Incarnation representing them in his own person. Christ thus, as the embodiment of the new Israel, the one true Israelite, is the first to receive the promised blessing and becomes the channel through which those who commit themselves to him in faith, whether Jews or Gentiles, likewise share in the benefits which God had from the beginning prepared for his people.

17. Returning to his argument, Paul now points out that the terms of the promise made by God to Abraham could not be affected by the promulgation of the Law, which after all only came into existence several centuries later. Paul gives the actual length of time between Abraham and Moses as 430 years, following the Greek version of Exod. 12: 40. Our Revised Version, based on the Hebrew text, gives 430 years as merely the time that the Israelites spent in Egypt. It matters little either way from Paul's point of view, since what he is contending for is that the terms of the promise must take precedence over the terms of the Law. The prior covenant is the one that must stand.

18. But God's covenant with Abraham, with its accompanying promise, was not a matter of law. This might be said about the covenant with Moses, where God undertook to bless the Israelites provided they adhered to the terms of the Law. God's promise to Abraham, however, was made as an act of pure grace without conditions. The blessing that was to come to Abraham's 'issue' was thus not a matter of *legal right* that his racial descendants, the Jews, could regard as something to which they were entitled. ✶

THE PURPOSE OF THE LAW

Then what of the law? It was added to make wrongdoing 19 a legal offence. It was a temporary measure pending the arrival of the 'issue' to whom the promise was made. It was promulgated through angels, and there was an intermediary; but an intermediary is not needed for one 20 party acting alone, and God is one.

✳ 19. Paul is throughout this section of his letter fencing with his unseen opponents who have in his view an exaggerated estimate of the importance of the Law. He now anticipates the question they would doubtless next want to ask. If what really matters is faith, and if it is through committing their lives to Christ that Christians, whether from a Jewish or a Gentile background, now receive the blessing promised to Abraham, what is the status of the Law which has dominated the life of the Jewish people for so many centuries, which was not so long ago considered by Paul himself to be the only way of salvation and which is still held in the highest esteem by the apostles and Jewish Christians in general?

Paul's answer is that the Law was introduced as *a temporary measure* for a particular purpose. That purpose was to make men aware of their shortcomings by setting up the standards which God expected and required of his people, to remind the Israelites of their obligations to God and their neighbours, and to exact penalties for non-compliance. In his letter to the Romans Paul goes further and says that from his own experience the Law actually encouraged wrongdoing by putting ideas into people's heads (Rom. 7: 7 ff.). Here, however, he says it has outlived its usefulness since the coming of Christ. Through him our relationship to God is no longer one of obedience but of love. Since his advent the blessing promised to Abraham is available through Christ for all his people. We are living in a new situation.

Moreover, says Paul, there is no comparison between the giving of the Law to Moses and the giving of the promise to Abraham. In the former case, as we are told, Moses received the Law indirectly from God, whereas Abraham received the promise, as it were, face to face. Paul refers here to the tradition which had grown up, and which is dependent on the Greek version of Deut. 33: 2, that at the giving of the Law on Mt Sinai, the Lord was accompanied by a host of angels who were responsible for transmitting the Law to Moses.

No doubt basically the idea was originally to emphasize the

majesty and remoteness of God. It was referred to in this positive sense by Stephen in his speech at his trial in Acts 7: 53 and by the author of Hebrews (2: 2 ff.) in the same derogatory sense as Paul refers to it here. Paul's point is that any word which came from God via his angels, and from them through a third party, or *intermediary*, namely Moses, to Israel, was obviously of less importance than a direct word spoken by God to Abraham himself, the father of all Israelites, as was the case with the promise.

20. The curious afterthought in verse 20 has been taken by many commentators to be a marginal note by some early scribe who was trying to make Paul's reasoning a little clearer. If this is so, he has not succeeded. What the words seem to mean is that in the case of a two-sided bargain, like the Law, an *intermediary* was essential, but in the case of a straight-forward promise, like that to Abraham, no third party was necessary. ✶

Does the law, then, contradict the promises? No, never! 21 If a law had been given which had power to bestow life, then indeed righteousness would have come from keeping the law. But Scripture has declared the whole world to 22 be prisoners in subjection to sin, so that faith in Jesus Christ may be the ground on which the promised blessing is given, and given to those who have such faith.

✶ 21. Paul as a good Jewish Christian could not possibly have said that the Law and the promises were in opposition. That would have meant denying the divine inspiration of the Old Testament and even suggesting that God did not know his own mind. He knew the words of Deut. 30: 15–20, that love of God and obedience to his commandments are the way to life. Perhaps also he knew the words of Jesus to the same effect (Matt. 19: 17). But the Law as Paul knew it was something different. It was not a liberating, life-giving concept but a deadening repressive body of enactments which cast a shadow over all human attempts to get right with God.

Paul from his own experience knew that as a punctilious Pharisee his attempt to adhere to the letter of the Law had brought only frustration and a deep sense of the gulf between himself and God. His obvious conclusion was that *righteousness*, i.e. the right relationship with God, could not come from observing in detail the terms of the Law. But he did not need to rely on his own experience to prove this. Again meeting his opponents on their own ground, he could find scriptural evidence to prove his point.

22. Already in 2: 16 and 3: 10 he has produced Old Testament backing for his claim that men left to themselves are helpless in the grip of sin, or as we might say today, unable to defeat their own selfish impulses. The twist in our natures cannot be straightened out by us unaided. In Rom. 3: 10–18 Paul gathers together a patchwork of Old Testament quotations which bear out this dismal conclusion. But the sequel is far from dismal, for it is this very failure of man to raise himself out of his self-made morass which in God's plan for our salvation Christ came to rectify. It is by committing ourselves in total allegiance to Christ that the right relationship to God which was in effect *the promised blessing* becomes a reality. ✳

NEW MEN IN CHRIST

23 Before this faith came, we were close prisoners in the
24 custody of law, pending the revelation of faith. Thus the law was a kind of tutor in charge of us until Christ should
25 come, when he should be justified through faith; and now that faith has come, the tutor's charge is at an end.
26   For through faith you are all sons of God in union with
27 Christ Jesus. Baptized into union with him, you have all

put on Christ as a garment. There is no such thing as Jew 28
and Greek, slave and freeman, male and female; for you
are all one person in Christ Jesus. But if you thus belong 29
to Christ, you are the 'issue' of Abraham, and so heirs by
promise.

* 23. Paul's basic picture of man's plight before the coming
of Christ is of the whole human race bound in chains forged
by its own folly and failure. Life could only be made tolerable
for society as a whole by the restraining power of law. Man
had to be kept in some kind of order by fear of the consequences of wrongdoing, by a rigid disciplinary code of
regulations, by warnings and penalties. But this was not life
as life was meant to be lived. Man was created in the image of
God and God intended him to be a son and not a slave. Now
in God's providence this had become a possibility. The new
kind of relationship to God which was now open to all who
committed themselves to Christ liberated men from *the
custody of the law*, freed them from its restraints and made its
protection no longer necessary.

24–5. Paul compares the function of the Law to that of a
tutor. The word he employs was used of household servants
who were responsible for looking after the sons of the family
until they reached years of manhood. Their duties were more
disciplinary than educational. It was their business to check
bad behaviour and generally to see that their young charges
came to no harm. When the boys 'came of age' the super-
visor's task was at an end. So the Law had served its purpose,
since it was no longer necessary to treat as recalcitrant
children men who had now entered into the full freedom of
life in Christ.

26–7. What then did this 'coming of age' mean for the
Christian? It meant that any man who accepted Christ as
Lord of his life became one of God's sons, united to Christ
who was God's Son in a unique sense. The sign and seal of

this unity of sonship between Christ and all Christians is baptism. This is no mere outward symbol of a change of heart but an act whereby the Christian is incorporated into Christ and becomes part of him. Paul speaks of baptism as 'putting on' Christ *as a garment*, just as the Old Testament talks of Job being clothed with righteousness (Job 29: 14) or of God being 'clothed with honour and majesty' (Ps. 104: 1). In all these cases what is involved is identification. Job becomes identified with righteousness; the very nature of God is honour and majesty. So by baptism the Christian becomes one with Christ. He is no longer his old self but a new self, since the spirit of Christ is at work within him.

28. For people who share this new life in Christ, the ordinary distinctions that society makes are no longer ultimate. Differences in class, race, colour and sex are obviously real differences and are not obliterated when men and women become Christians. But they are seen in a different light. We recognize that, in the sight of God, company director and office-boy, Bantu and white South African, Asian and European are of equal value. Not only so, but when men and women in all their human variety become Christians they are caught up into a new unity of fellowship with Christ and with one another.

29. This means that all Christians—but of course the Galatians are primarily in the apostle's mind—whatever their background or upbringing, are entitled to the blessing promised by God to Abraham and his '*issue*'. We are all Abraham's children by virtue of our faith-union with Christ, who was Abraham's true offspring since he was the one true Israelite. We therefore receive the benefits which God decreed should come to the nations through the historical channel which he appointed, the people of Israel, now reconstituted as the new Israel, the new People of God, the Christian Church. ✳

This is what I mean: so long as the heir is a minor, he is **4**
no better off than a slave, even though the whole estate
is his; he is under guardians and trustees until the date 2
fixed by his father. And so it was with us. During our 3
minority we were slaves to the elemental spirits of the
universe, but when the term was completed, God sent 4
his own Son, born of a woman, born under the law, to 5
purchase freedom for the subjects of the law, in order that
we might attain the status of sons.

✶ 1–2. A new thought strikes Paul at this point, probably
suggested by what he has just said about 'heirs'. He has
already spoken of life governed by the Law as being like
the life of children in charge of a household slave (3: 24);
now he says that before the coming of Christ Jews and Gentiles
alike were no better off than slaves themselves. Before a boy
comes to the age when he is entitled to inherit what has been
willed to him by his father, he is under the thumb of those who
have been put in charge of his upbringing or who have been
appointed to look after his property. He is not a free agent. So
although mankind in the providence of God was one day
destined to be offered the rich inheritance that belongs to God's
sons, it had to pass through a stage which was akin to slavery.

3. Paul describes this state of human existence as a time
when life was dominated by *the elemental spirits of the universe*.
It seems an astonishing thing to say, since he is obviously
speaking of Jews as well as Gentiles. Astrology, that is, the
belief that human life is affected by the stars, was a common
feature of pagan religion in Paul's day—and, we might add,
in our own day too. The natural world was thought to be
ruled by a hierarchy of good and evil spirits, angels and
demons, who inhabited or controlled sun, moon and stars
and through them influenced men's destinies.

Paul had no doubt of the existence of demonic powers in the universe. But for him they were something to be fought against, not worshipped (Eph. 6: 12). Gentiles who had become Christians were freed from the tyranny of these unknowable and inexplicable powers which ruled their existence. But how can Paul put the Law which dominated the life of the Jews in the same category? Some commentators have got over the difficulty by assuming that the Greek word here translated 'elemental spirits' means 'elementary ideas'. This is a possible meaning, and would suggest that Paul is speaking of Jewish religion and Gentile religion as being religions of immaturity, suitable for mankind at a stage in its development before it was given the full knowledge of the truth about the meaning of life by the coming of Christ. This sense of the word, however, would not fit in with what the apostle goes on to say in verses 8 and 9.

It is clear, therefore, that what Paul means is that both paganism and Judaism are religions which make men slaves. They are subject to external compulsion, they live in fear of inadvertently doing something wrong, they are helpless victims of an arbitrary power. Whether Paul had in mind the idea he has already referred to (3: 19) that the Law was originally transmitted through angelic beings, or whether he thought of the attitude of the rigorists towards the Law as being little different from idolatry, it is obvious that he felt that there was little to choose between the plight of Jews and that of Gentiles before the advent of Christ.

4–5. But with the Incarnation the whole human situation was transformed. The day of man's servitude was past. The day of man's liberation had dawned. It happened, as Paul says, *when the term was completed*, i.e. the term of man's *minority* before he entered into his full status of sonship and inherited what his heavenly Father intended him to have. Perhaps the more familiar translation in the Revised Version suggests more vividly the crucial character of this great moment in the divine drama: 'when the fulness of the time came, God sent forth his Son.'

IN THE FULNESS OF THE TIME

The apostle is thinking of his analogy of the boy who lives under the control of guardians until *the date fixed by his father* (verse 2). God and God alone decided that the time was ripe for the coming of Christ. But God, as Paul would be the first to say, never does anything without good reason even if we cannot see the reason fully at the time. As we look back, however, to the point in history when Christ was born and the Good News was proclaimed, we can see in what a wonderful way the ground had been prepared.

There was the legacy of the faith and morality of Israel, which had already made an impact on the pagan world through the synagogues of the Jews scattered throughout the Roman Empire. There was the quest of thoughtful pagans for some new answer to the problems of life, other than the hollowness of temple cults and the barrenness of philosophers' ethics. For the first time there was a basic language, colloquial Greek, which Paul himself, the gospel writers and any missionary could use to spread the message from end to end of the civilized world. Rome provided the great imperial roads, guaranteed peaceful transit to teachers of the new faith, and by her tolerance of religious beliefs was to give the young Church a chance to grow and spread.

It was at this providentially strategic time in the long story of man's development that *God sent his own Son*. Jesus was not for Paul primarily the Messiah of the Jews but the Son of God, 'begotten of his Father before all worlds', who came from God and returned to him. The full measure of Paul's thought on this point can be seen in Phil. 2: 6–11. Yet this divine, pre-existent Son was *born of a woman*, that is, entered into our human situation as one of ourselves. This is a common biblical expression denoting ordinary manhood (cf. Job 14: 1; Matt. 11: 11).

Jesus was, moreover, *born under the law*, not only as a man of a particular race, at a particular time and in a particular place, but as one who shared the frustration of being subjected to the domination of the very system from which he came to deliver us. He became a slave so that we might be free. Paul has already explained (3: 13) how Christ by his Death and Resurrection had liberated the Jews from the thraldom of the Law, and what he had done for Israel he had done in principle for all mankind. So all of us who by committing our lives to Christ in faith become part of his Body, the new Israel, are no longer slaves but sons. The *status* of sonship, which Christ had by right of being the unique Son of God, is granted to us by virtue of what he has done. ✶

ABBA! FATHER!

6 To prove that you are sons, God has sent into our hearts
7 the Spirit of his Son, crying 'Abba! Father!' You are therefore no longer a slave but a son, and if a son, then also by God's own act an heir.

8 Formerly, when you did not acknowledge God, you were the slaves of beings which in their nature are no
9 gods. But now that you do acknowledge God—or rather, now that he has acknowledged you—how can you turn back to the mean and beggarly spirits of the elements? Why do you propose to enter their service all over again?
10 You keep special days and months and seasons and years.
11 You make me fear that all the pains I spent on you may prove to be labour lost.

✶ 6–7. Sometimes, when he speaks of what Christ has done for us, Paul seems almost to be thinking of a legal transaction. These last verses 1–5 are a case in point. But as if he were aware of that danger, he hastens to correct any misunderstanding. Paul's theology is basically one of personal relationships—new relationships which have become possible between

God and ourselves and between ourselves and others because of Christ. What Christ has done is not to make a book entry in a divine ledger, which balances up what we have failed to do with what he has done on our behalf. Paul now shows that the result of what Christ has done is essentially not to give us a new *status* but a new attitude to God.

We are not now dealing with the unpredictable effects of the stars on our destinies, or with a remote and forbidding lawgiver with inexorable demands, but with one who is still the author and creator of all that is, but whom we can now call our dear Father. The word *Abba* brings us very close to Jesus. It is the Aramaic word for father which he used himself in his prayers (cf. Mark 14: 36). It is what a Jewish boy would have affectionately called his own father. Jesus has taught us, in stories like the Prodigal Son, to think of God in just this way, and it is his *Spirit* within us that enables us to speak to God in these terms in our prayers. So our own experience confirms that we are indeed sons and not slaves, inheriting the blessings which our Heavenly Father has destined for his children.

8–9. Having built up his case that through Christ the true relationship between God and man has been made plain, the apostle now speaks directly to the Galatian situation. He reminds them of their pre-Christian days when they believed they were at the mercy of demonic beings who decided their fate. How can they possibly now turn their backs on the God they have come to know, or rather the God who has sought them out, and revert to the kind of pagan worship of the stars from which they have so recently escaped?

10. For this, says Paul, is what their new-found enthusiasm for Jewish practices amounts to. He does not mention circumcision here, which was the main issue, but pinpoints Judaism's addiction to the celebration of special *days* (like the sabbath), *months* (the 'new moons' that Isaiah ridiculed— Isa. 1: 14), *seasons* (like the Passover) and *years* (presumably the sabbatical year referred to in Lev. 25). Since all these

observances, dear to the heart of the Jewish-Christian extremists, depend on astronomical calculations, they spring in the last resort from the same kind of superstition as heathenism. Paul is not of course dismissing all religious festivals as meaningless—as we learn from Acts, they meant a great deal to him—but when they become the beginning and end of religion they are, as the Old Testament prophets always insisted, a travesty of true worship. Aids to devotion, yes, but the heart of the gospel, no. ✳

PAUL RECALLS THE CAMPAIGN

12 Put yourselves in my place, my brothers, I beg you, for I have put myself in yours. It is not that you did me any
13 wrong. As you know, it was bodily illness that originally
14 led to my bringing you the Gospel, and you resisted any temptation to show scorn or disgust at the state of my poor body; you welcomed me as if I were an angel of God, as you might have welcomed Christ Jesus himself.
15 Have you forgotten how happy you thought yourselves in having me with you? I can say this for you: you would have torn out your very eyes, and given them to me,
16 had that been possible! And have I now made myself your enemy by being honest with you?
17 The persons I have referred to are envious of you, but not with an honest envy: what they really want is to bar
18 the door to you so that you may come to envy them. It is always a fine thing to deserve an honest envy—always,
19 and not only when I am present with you, dear children. For my children you are, and I am in travail with you
20 over again until you take the shape of Christ. I wish I could be with you now; then I could modify my tone; as it is, I am at my wits' end about you.

✻ Paul is so moved at this point in his letter that he breaks off his argument and makes a direct personal appeal to his readers, recalling the circumstances of his visit to Galatia. Not everything that he refers to is crystal clear to us, though it must have been so to his recalcitrant flock. He asks them (verse 12) to try to understand his own position in the matter, and to share it, just as in his Galatian campaign he was prepared as a Jew to meet them as Gentiles on their own ground. He is not accusing them of any hostile act (verse 13). But he is grieved at the contrast between their attitude then and their attitude now.

We have already traced the probable course of events that led to Paul's initial visit to the people to whom he is writing (pp. 1–2). Malaria seems to fit the description he gives in verse 14 better than ophthalmia or epilepsy, particularly since those who suffered from malaria were regarded in Asia Minor as under the curse of the gods. As we have seen, the reference to his reception as *an angel of God* fits in with Luke's narrative in Acts 14: 11. During the mission the Galatians had treated him almost with adulation. When Paul says *you would have torn out your very eyes and given them to me* it does not necessarily mean that his eyesight was affected by his illness. It is probably merely a graphic way of saying: 'There was nothing that you would not have done for me.' Surely this wonderful relationship between the missionary and his converts cannot now be destroyed by straight talking (verses 15–16).

The trouble-makers in Galatia are playing an underhand game. They are trying to make the Galatians feel that they are second-class Christians who must conform with Jewish law in order to qualify for full status (verse 17). It is not that the apostle is jealous of these people with their smooth tongues (verse 18). All that he is passionately concerned about is that his converts, whom he thinks of as his children, should become full-grown men and women in Christ (verse 19). If he were only able to talk to them instead of writing, things would be so much easier. He could judge the situation on the spot and deal with it, instead of worrying himself frantic (verse 20). This is an extraordinarily revealing glimpse of Paul as a father in God. ✳

HAGAR AND SARAH

21 Tell me now, you who are so anxious to be under law,
22 will you not listen to what the Law says? It is written there that Abraham had two sons, one by his slave and
23 the other by his free-born wife. The slave-woman's son was born in the course of nature, the free woman's
24 through God's promise. This is an allegory. The two women stand for two covenants. The one bearing children into slavery is the covenant that comes from Mount
25 Sinai: that is Hagar. Sinai is a mountain in Arabia and it represents the Jerusalem of today, for she and her children
26 are in slavery. But the heavenly Jerusalem is the free
27 woman; she is our mother. For Scripture says, 'Rejoice, O barren woman who never bore child; break into a shout of joy, you who never knew a mother's pangs; for the deserted wife shall have more children than she who lives with the husband.'

28 And you, my brothers, like Isaac, are children of God's
29 promise. But just as in those days the natural-born son
30 persecuted the spiritual son, so it is today. But what does Scripture say? 'Drive out the slave-woman and her son, for the son of the slave shall not share the inheritance with
31 the free woman's son.' You see, then, my brothers, we are no slave-woman's children; our mother is the free
5 woman. Christ set us free, to be free men. Stand firm, then, and refuse to be tied to the yoke of slavery again.

⁎ After his direct appeal to the Galatians (verses 12–20), the apostle rounds off the doctrinal section of his letter (chapters 3–4) with what on the face of it seems to be a masterpiece of irrelevancy from the modern point of view. We tend nowadays to be suspicious of any attempt to side-step the plain meaning of Old Testament incidents by treating them as allegorical. It is too easy to make things mean just what you want them to mean. This passage is no exception. Paul's opponents could have taken the same Old Testament story and drawn the opposite conclusion by using the same allegorical method.

It is best therefore to look first at the point Paul is trying to make, which of course does not depend on his allegory or indeed on any particular scriptural texts at all. He is re-emphasizing what he has already said, that Judaism is a religion based on the Law, while Christianity is a religion based on God's promises. Life lived under the Law is slavery, life lived in response to God's promised blessing in Christ is freedom. He adds now that Judaism is doomed to perish, even if for a time its devotees are in a position to make things difficult for Christ's people.

With this in mind, we can regard Paul's use of allegory as an illustration of his main thesis, couched in the manner of the times and apt enough for the kind of audience he is addressing, if not very convincing to us. He takes the story in Gen. 16 ff. of Abraham's two sons, Ishmael and Isaac, the former the result of Abraham's union with Hagar, Sarah's maid, and the latter the unexpected child of his old age by his hitherto barren wife as a result of God's promise that she would have a son. Paul interprets this in a way which must have enraged his Jewish antagonists.

Hagar, the slave-woman, he says, represents the old covenant made through Moses on Mt Sinai, a mountain in Arabia, a land of bondage, as Jerusalem was in Paul's day under its Roman rulers. The Jews are therefore to be bracketed with Ishmael, as children of slavery. Sarah, on the other hand, the free woman, represents the new covenant, which is based on the promise to Abraham, which by-passes the covenant on Sinai, and which is fulfilled in Christ. She also stands for the heavenly Jerusalem, the true home of Christ's people. Christians are therefore to be bracketed with Isaac, as children of freedom.

Paul quotes two Old Testament texts in verses 27 and 30 to strengthen his case. Isaiah, he implies, was really speaking of the heavenly Jerusalem and prophesying the growth of the Church (Isa: 54: 1), whereas the sentence of banishment pronounced in Gen. 21: 10 on Hagar and Ishmael foretells the end of Judaism. This is all pretty far-fetched, although no doubt it was an effective argument at a time when this kind of allegorical use of Scripture was accepted as legitimate. It does not invalidate Paul's basic contention, summed up in the concluding words of this passage, that Christianity is good news of the liberation of the human spirit through Christ from all the forces that seek to enslave it, or his appeal to all Christians to resist any attempts to turn it into a religion of slavish obedience to rules and regulations. The life of Christians is the response of loving sons to a loving Father, whose service is perfect freedom. ✲

5: 2-25 LIBERTY NOT LICENCE

2 Mark my words: I, Paul, say to you that if you receive
3 circumcision Christ will do you no good at all. Once again, you can take it from me that every man who receives circumcision is under obligation to keep the
4 entire law. When you seek to be justified by way of law, your relation with Christ is completely severed: you have
5 fallen out of the domain of God's grace. For to us, our hope of attaining that righteousness which we eagerly
6 await is the work of the Spirit through faith. If we are in union with Christ Jesus circumcision makes no difference

at all, nor does the want of it; the only thing that counts is faith active in love.

LAW AND GRACE

✻ 2. After the involved symbolism of the allegory of Hagar and Sarah, this straightforward presentation of the issues at stake in the Galatian situation comes like a breath of fresh air. Paul throws down the gauntlet, as it were, and challenges his readers to face up to the implications of their attitude. This is not, he says in effect, a minor matter where, out of respect for long-standing tradition, Christians acknowledge that since their roots are in the faith and practice of the Old Testament they can happily incorporate some Jewish elements into their religious life.

He has earlier (4: 10) spoken of the Galatians' obsession with the observance of holy days and sacred festivals. The point at issue, however, is much more radical. It strikes at the very heart of what it means to be a Christian. If, says Paul, we start from the position that a Christian is someone who has committed his life to Christ, acknowledging him as Saviour and Lord, there can be no other absolute requirement. The Jewish-Christian agitators in Galatia were not claiming merely that circumcision was a 'good thing'. If they had done so, Paul, as a Jewish Christian himself, would have agreed with them. The difference between them was that Paul would have said circumcision was right for Christians who had been brought up in the Jewish tradition, but completely irrelevant for any other kind of Christians.

It was an ancient practice, hallowed by centuries of loyal observance, meaningful in a particular historical setting in that it bound together the sons of Israel as the special channel of God's revelation before the coming of Christ. Since the coming of Christ, loyalty to race, tradition and religious heritage made circumcision still a proper practice for Christians of Jewish extraction. But it must be no more than that. Neither must it be treated as a religious fetish nor must this external act, however rich in meaning, be equated in importance with the act of allegiance, involving the whole personality, whereby a man handed over his life to God as he had come to know him in Jesus Christ.

From the actual words Paul uses here, it is not clear whether some of the non-Jewish members of the churches in Galatia had already been so influenced by the pertinacity of the Jewish-Christian extremists that they were seriously considering submitting to circumcision. They have apparently not done so yet. What the apostle is insisting on, with all the force that words can convey, is that in the form in which this demand is being presented by the rigorists it is totally inadmissible. Full membership of Christ's Church, the status of being incorporated into the new Israel, depends on our relationship to Christ and not on compliance with any allegedly essential ecclesiastical qualification.

3. Moreover, adds the apostle, there can be no half measures. Those who accede to the demand of the rigorists and agree to circumcision must be prepared to comply with the Law in its entirety. Whatever obligations the Jewish legal code demands, however trivial and, in a non-Palestinian setting, however irrelevant, must be strictly observed. We may take it from his words here that even on the occasion of his initial missionary campaign Paul had warned the Galatians of the logical consequences of dabbling in Judaism.

4. The basic contention of the Judaizers was that only by circumcision could any Christian be certain that he was indeed a member of the historical people of God, destined to receive the blessings that God had promised to Israel through Abraham. Paul's point is that Judaism and Christianity do not talk the same language. Judaism makes the right relationship with God and incorporation into his people dependent on compliance with an external rite. Christianity is a religion of *grace*, demanding only that we accept the mercy and forgiveness of God freely offered in Christ. When we make this

venture of faith, we embark on a relationship with Christ in which legalism has no place. So, here is the apostle's stern warning that any departure from this basic position means that the relationship is broken: we cut ourselves off from Christ.

5–6. The only *hope* we have, continues Paul, of ever coming to the full knowledge of God, of realising our full status as sons of God and of being fit to stand in his presence hereafter, rests on what God does for us and within us now by the power of his *Spirit* in response to our commitment of ourselves wholly to him in faith. Fundamentally, all that matters in the life of a Christian is to be *in union with Christ Jesus,* committed to him in loyalty and obedience, in trust and gratitude. This is what is meant by *faith* and it is bound to work out in loving service of our fellow men. In the light of this, circumcision—or indeed any other external requirement —is a matter of indifference. It does not count one way or the other. That a devout and patriotic Jew should have reached this amazing conclusion is a measure of the depth of Paul's Christian insight and of his spiritual journey since he watched Stephen being stoned to death. ✻

THE TROUBLE-MAKERS

You were running well; who was it hindered you from 7 following the truth? Whatever persuasion he used, it did 8 not come from God who is calling you; 'a little leaven', 9 remember, 'leavens all the dough'. United with you in 10 the Lord, I am confident that you will not take the wrong view; but the man who is unsettling your minds, whoever he may be, must bear God's judgement. And I, my friends, 11 if I am still advocating circumcision, why is it I am still persecuted? In that case, my preaching of the cross is a stumbling-block no more. As for these agitators, they had 12 better go the whole way and make eunuchs of themselves!

✳ 7–9. After his great pronouncement in verse 6, Paul now utters some home truths about the trouble-makers in the Galatian congregations. What has come over the young churches, he asks. What has checked their steady growth in Christian witness and service when everything was going so well? Paul, who obviously is in the dark about the identity of the agitators, has no doubt that they, rather than the church members, are to blame. People have been too easily influenced and have been prepared to listen to these rigorists as if they were preaching the word of God. Paul reminds them of the Jewish proverb which amounts to saying that a drop of ink can discolour a whole glass of water. Except when Jesus talks of the growth of the Kingdom of God being like yeast in dough (Matt. 13: 33), the Bible generally uses the word *leaven* in a bad sense, as Paul does here.

10–12. Yet, as so often, the apostle refuses to believe that his flock will be permanently led astray. He is convinced of this because he knows that the hand of God is in their common venture in Christian fellowship. Nevertheless, whoever it is who is causing the trouble among them will have to answer to God for it. Incredible though it may seem, Paul is apparently being accused of *still advocating circumcision*, i.e. supporting the claim of those who said that Gentiles must become 'sons of Abraham' by circumcision before they could be classed as proper Christians.

What grounds there could be for such an insinuation it is difficult to see. Admittedly Paul insisted on circumcision in the case of Timothy, who was half a Jew (Acts 16: 3), and there seems to have been some misrepresentation of his attitude in the case of Titus who was a full Gentile (see note on 2: 3). But as Paul says here, his opponents cannot have it both ways. If he is still implying by his words or actions that circumcision is essential for all Christians, why is he still being attacked by the rigorists in Galatia? Surely what they held against him was just that the heart of his message was that salvation for both Jews and Gentiles depended now on what Christ had done, above all by his death, and not on circumcision or observance of the Law. If this was not the reason for their opposition, surely what he was preaching about the *cross* could not give them any cause for complaint. They could no longer regard it as a *stumbling-block*. Then in a very human outburst Paul gives vent to his feelings. Why do these enthusiasts for circumcision not go the whole hog and get themselves castrated and thus *make eunuchs of themselves* like some of the pagan priests? ✻

CHRISTIAN FREEDOM

You, my friends, were called to be free men; only do 13 not turn your freedom into licence for your lower nature, but be servants to one another in love. For the 14 whole law can be summed up in a single commandment: 'Love your neighbour as yourself.' But if you go on 15 fighting one another, tooth and nail, all you can expect is mutual destruction.

✻ 13. From this point almost to the end of the letter (6: 10), Paul is dealing with the practical implications of the doctrine of Christian freedom which he has been expounding in the last two chapters. God intends, as the apostle has just been telling us, that every Christian man should be free to live his life without being hemmed in by a host of prohibitions and restrictions, and without feeling that he is at the mercy of some malignant fate which controls his destiny. But there is also the danger, inherent in Paul's doctrine, that the nature of that freedom may be misunderstood. It certainly does not mean that a Christian is free to do what he likes. That is to confuse freedom with *licence*.

Paul is not necessarily thinking of sexual licence when he speaks of our giving in to our *lower nature*. He means self-centredness in any shape or form. The keynote of true Christian freedom is a readiness to serve others. Indeed the word Paul uses for *servants* is the same as the word for slaves. We escape from slavish dependence on arbitrary authority in order that we may become willing slaves of one another in mutual love.

14–15. To those who would extol the virtues of the Law of Moses—and it had many splendid precepts to which the apostle would wholeheartedly have subscribed—he quotes the words from Leviticus 19: 18 which Jesus himself had used (Mark 12: 29–31) as the essence of the Law and the heart of its teaching: *Love your neighbour as yourself.* As Paul says elsewhere (Rom. 13: 10): 'the whole law is summed up in love.' But the wrangling that was going on in the Galatian churches, no doubt about the pros and cons of Judaism, was the negation of love and the death-knell of Christian brotherhood. ✷

THE GUIDANCE OF THE SPIRIT

16 I mean this: if you are guided by the Spirit you will not
17 fulfil the desires of your lower nature. That nature sets its desires against the Spirit, while the Spirit fights against it. They are in conflict with one another so that what you
18 will to do you cannot do. But if you are led by the Spirit, you are not under law.

✷ 16. Paul has just mentioned in verse 15 the acrimonious controversy which was destroying the peace of the Galatian churches. This leads him on to a general statement about the differences that ought to exist between Christians and non-Christians.

All of us start off from scratch with a motley collection of instincts and impulses, with the dominant desire to do the best we can for ourselves and make the most of the chances life offers. Our natural inclination is to do so no matter what the cost may be to others or what casualties we leave in our wake. When it is left to ourselves within the limits imposed by the state, or even in defiance of them, we follow the law of the jungle—every man for himself. Those who recognize that there is a higher authority and a greater good than self-enrichment, whether that recognition comes through the teaching of the various religions or a variety of philosophies, come to see the difference between good and evil, between self-fulfilment and self-aggrandizement. They would sub-scribe to Paul's view, though not necessarily in the same words, that we all 'fall short of the glory of God' (Rom. 3: 23, Revised Version), and that to get the most out of life in the fullest sense we have to take ourselves in hand and not give in to what Paul calls the *desires* of our *lower nature*.

Christians, however, have a distinctive view of the matter in that they believe that they are not left to themselves to fight this battle. Since the gift of the Spirit was given to the Church at Pentecost (Acts 2), there is a power available to help men and women who try to live their lives in accordance with the pattern set by Jesus, which they accept as God's will for themselves and the rest of the world. If Christians offer their hearts and minds to the Spirit of God within the fellow-ship of the Church, in worship, in prayer, in sacrament, and in the study of the Scriptures, then they are consciously or unconsciously letting themselves be *guided by the Spirit*. How far this affects their behaviour depends on how serious they are about what it means to be a Christian.

17. If they are in earnest about their membership of the Church, they know that there is a constant tension within themselves between what they want to do and what they ought to do. What they want to do is generally something that is either easier or appears to be more immediately rewarding. It is seldom if ever the thing that is most costly. Yet they know in their hearts that self-sacrifice is the very essence of the Christian life. They are under discipline, in a

sense, but it is a discipline which is accepted not as a tyrannical interference with personal liberty, but in acknowledgement of the fact that without self-discipline there is little to distinguish men from animals. This is why Paul says to us, *what you will to do you cannot do*. The Spirit, in other words, stops you from doing it.

18. But, Paul would add, this is something quite different from being *under law*. If we abstain from certain types of behaviour because we are striving to stick to the regulations of some prescribed legal code—for example, if we avoid stealing money in case we should be found out and punished—this is not a truly Christian motive. A Christian will not steal money from his neighbour, because the power of the Spirit keeps him in the Christian way, so that the idea of stealing just does not enter his head. Therefore, Paul would argue, we must always let ourselves be *led by the Spirit*. ✳

THE HARVEST OF THE SPIRIT

19 Anyone can see the kind of behaviour that belongs to the lower nature: fornication, impurity, and indecency;
20 idolatry and sorcery; quarrels, a contentious temper, envy, fits of rage, selfish ambitions, dissensions, party
21 intrigues, and jealousies; drinking bouts, orgies, and the like. I warn you, as I warned you before, that those who behave in such ways will never inherit the kingdom of God.

22 But the harvest of the Spirit is love, joy, peace, patience,
23 kindness, goodness, fidelity, gentleness, and self-control. There is no law dealing with such things as these.
24 And those who belong to Christ Jesus have crucified
25 the lower nature with its passions and desires. If the Spirit is the source of our life, let the Spirit also direct our course.

* 19–21. Having established the fact that there is a constant tussle going on inside us between our animal instincts and selfish impulses on the one hand, and, on the other, the power of the Spirit seeking to make us better sons and daughters of God, Paul goes on now to list some of the results when we allow one or other to win. First, he instances the types of conduct that spring from surrender to our *lower nature*. They are the sort of things that most of us are ready to condemn at once in other people but not always in ourselves. We may avoid the blatant sexual sins and drunken orgies, but the list also includes bad temper, jealousy and selfish ambition.

It is not important to try to classify the offences in Paul's list. Many of them are common targets of moralists in any day and age. Others are perhaps more relevant to the situation in a first-century pagan city—for example, *idolatry* and *sorcery*, although twentieth-century man is not without his own idols (e.g. status symbols), or his belief in magic (e.g. horoscopes). Paul here reinforces the message that he had originally delivered in Galatia, that the Christian life is as much a matter of behaviour as of right belief. Faith and conduct are two sides of the same coin. The choices that we make every day, Paul tells us, are of vital moment, for they affect our life hereafter. Christians have no automatic entry into the presence of God.

22–23. On the other hand, if we let our lives be completely guided by the Spirit of God, the lovely qualities that the apostle goes on now to list are certain to become ours. But we have only to read the list and then look at ourselves to see how little scope we allow the Spirit in our day-to-day existence. Yet Paul rightly says that these splendid characteristics ought to be the hallmark of any Christian who takes his faith seriously. We can be encouraged by the fact that on the whole we see more of these qualities among Christians than among any other group in society, even if the total picture that the Church presents falls lamentably below the standard on every count.

23–5. The lives of the Christian saints are historical evidence of the truth of Paul's words. For apart from Christ, of whom Paul's *harvest of the Spirit* might be a personal description, only saints approximate to these requirements. Such a quality of living, as Paul goes on to say, has nothing to do with striving to observe the terms of any set of rules. It comes from commitment to Christ and from that alone. Paul has already (2: 20) described in terms of 'crucifixion' the difference between his old life, before Christ took hold of him on the Damascus road, and his new life as a Christian. By identifying himself with Christ the old Paul died and the new Paul was born.

This for Paul was the pattern of Christian experience. By committing ourselves to Christ, and by baptism, we die symbolically to our past life and rise again to a new life which Christ lives in us. What Paul and the Christian saints experienced is beyond the ordinary run of Christian men and women, who know only too well how far they have yet to travel. But Christ has made it possible for us to begin the journey. His Spirit is a new element in our lives, and Paul urges us to keep our hearts and minds constantly open and responsive to him. ✻

5: 26 — 6: 18   LOVE IN ACTION

26 We must not be conceited, challenging one another to
6 rivalry, jealous of one another. If a man should do something wrong, my brothers, on a sudden impulse, you who are endowed with the Spirit must set him right again very gently. Look to yourself, each one of you: you
2 may be tempted too. Help one another to carry these heavy loads, and in this way you will fulfil the law of Christ.

3   For if a man imagines himself to be somebody, when
4 he is nothing, he is deluding himself. Each man should

examine his own conduct for himself; then he can measure his achievement by comparing himself with himself and not with anyone else. For everyone has his ₅ own proper burden to bear.

When anyone is under instruction in the faith, he ₆ should give his teacher a share of all good things he has.

* 5: 26. Chapter divisions were not introduced into the text of the Bible until the thirteenth century, and division into verses does not appear before the sixteenth century. Sometimes, therefore, it is purely a matter of the translator's judgement whether a verse belongs to the end of one chapter or the beginning of the next. Here, as in 5: 1, the N.E.B. departs from the chapter divisions of the R.V. It certainly seems that 5: 26 begins a new line of thought and hangs together with what now follows.

The apostle has been speaking of what happens when men and women allow themselves to be guided by the Spirit of Christ. He has painted a picture of what the Church would be like if all its members were saints. Now he turns to the Church as it is, a brotherhood of sinners who find it extraordinarily difficult to *become* saints. He speaks first of all of our temptation to be self-satisfied, provoking and envious, and then goes on to contrast this with the kind of attitude we would adopt towards a fellow Christian if we really let the Spirit rule our lives.

6: 1-2. There may be in this whole passage a special reference to certain circumstances in the Galatian situation about which we now know nothing, but the apostle's counsel is universally applicable. He singles out for particular mention the case of a church member who has yielded to sudden temptation. Paul's interpretation of what Jesus would have done in such a case involves neither expelling the man from the congregation nor sitting in judgement on him, but offering help and sympathy. We are all equally liable to go

GALATIANS 5: 26 — 6: 6   *Faith and Freedom*

astray, says Paul, and we can never tell the strength of another
man's temptation. The law of Christian love involves understanding and sharing each other's difficulties, and it is a law
which is far more demanding than any moral code.

3–5. One of the besetting temptations in the life of any of
us—especially if we are very conscious of some personal
failure—is to console ourselves with the reflexion that at least
we are not as bad as So-and-So. This is what Paul is condemn-
ing here; for this, however much we deny it, is the self-
righteousness of the Pharisee. As Christians we must judge
ourselves in comparison with Christ, and in the last resort we
are answerable for our actions to God alone, who knows what
is in our hearts and what we have to fight against.

6. As a further example of love in action, Paul touches
briefly on the responsibility of members of a Christian
community to support their minister. Paul's own practice
on his missionary tours was to pay his own way by working
at his trade as a tent-maker, fitting in his evangelistic work
as best he could (Acts 18: 1–3). Part at least of the reason for
this was that he could then refute any charges that he was in
the business simply for the money, like many itinerant
charlatans in his day (1 Thess. 2: 8–9).

It seems to have been his practice to second members of
his missionary team for limited periods to follow up the
initial campaign, as in the case of the Macedonian churches
where Silas and Timothy were left behind while Paul went
on to Athens and Corinth (Acts 17: 14; 18: 5). This temporary
arrangement was obviously not the final answer to the problem of building up a young Christian community, encouraging new inquirers, instructing intending members and
generally supervising the life and work of the congregations.

We are told in Acts 14: 23 that on leaving Galatia after
his first missionary tour Paul had appointed elders in each
of the churches that he had founded. Presumably some or all
of these are the teachers referred to here (verse 6). The words
imply that they had a full-time job and were not simply

teaching the faith in their spare moments. The apostle urges
his readers to recognize the right of the minister to be maintained by the congregation, and the duty of the members to
share in maintaining him. Paul followed the maxim of Jesus
that 'the worker earns his keep' (Matt. 10: 10; cf. 1 Cor.
9: 14). ⚹

THIS IS GOD'S WORLD

Make no mistake about this: God is not to be fooled; a 7
man reaps what he sows. If he sows seed in the field of 8
his lower nature, he will reap from it a harvest of cor-
ruption, but if he sows in the field of the Spirit, the Spirit
will bring him a harvest of eternal life. So let us never 9
tire of doing good, for if we do not slacken our efforts
we shall in due time reap our harvest. Therefore, as 10
opportunity offers, let us work for the good of all,
especially members of the household of the faith.

⚹ 7. Paul now rounds off what he has been saying since
5: 13, about the implications of Christian freedom and what it
means to be sons of God. The thought he wants to leave with
us is that we must be in earnest about what we do with our
lives because we have to reckon with God. We cannot play
fast and loose with the moral order of the universe. If we
abuse the freedom God gives us, and choose to disregard the
promptings of his Spirit, we pay the penalty sooner or later.
Paul's metaphor of sowing and reaping in verse 8, based on
the proverbial expression in verse 7, *a man reaps what he sows,*
is clearly not meant to be analysed for its horticultural
accuracy.

8–9. What the apostle is saying is that if we base our lives
on the principle that self comes first we shall end up, rotten to
the core, in spiritual death. If we let the Spirit of Jesus guide
our behaviour, the end-product is life as God meant it to be,
life lived in such a relationship to God that the death of the

body cannot destroy it. This is why, despite every discouragement and failure, we must persevere in the practice of charity and compassion with sympathy and goodwill, as Jesus has taught us. Since this is God's world, we may rest assured that if we do so, in the long run we shall reach the fulfilment of our life in the blessedness of his nearer presence.

10. So Paul urges us to lose no opportunity of Christian service, both in the world and in the Church. Paul's conception of Christian love in action sees nothing less than the whole world as our parish. In modern life that means a summons to us all, according to our gifts and bent, to work for the renewal of the life of society on all levels—in politics, social welfare, education, industry, commerce, in short, wherever we are involved or can be involved. But obviously the needs of the Church and its people, *the household of the faith*, will have a special place in our hearts. And although the obvious field of service will be within the branch of the Church to which we belong, Paul's passionate concern for the unity of the Body of Christ would dare us at our peril to limit our service to any one denomination. *

A FINAL SALVO

11 You see these big letters? I am now writing to you in my
12 own hand. It is all those who want to make a fair outward and bodily show who are trying to force circumcision upon you; their sole object is to escape persecution for
13 the cross of Christ. For even those who do receive circumcision are not thoroughgoing observers of the law: they only want you to be circumcised in order to
14 boast of your having submitted to that outward rite. But God forbid that I should boast of anything but the cross of our Lord Jesus Christ, through which the world is
15 crucified to me and I to the world! Circumcision is

nothing; uncircumcision is nothing; the only thing that counts is new creation! Whoever they are who take this 16 principle for their guide, peace and mercy be upon them, and upon the whole Israel of God!

In future let no one make trouble for me, for I bear the 17 marks of Jesus branded on my body.

The grace of our Lord Jesus Christ be with your spirit, 18 my brothers. Amen.

✳ 11. At this point Paul takes the pen from the scribe and writes a postscript in his own handwriting. His normal practice, as we can see from the conclusions of his various letters, was to dictate the whole epistle and then sometimes to add a greeting and always his signature (2 Thess. 3: 17). Here, to emphasize the point, he adds a paragraph in his own writing and in *big letters*, like a public notice, to mark the importance of what he is saying.

12. His last few words pinpoint the main issue of the letter and the apostle's main concern in writing it. This whole trouble in the Galatian churches, says Paul to his readers, this demand that all Christians must submit to the Old Testament rite of circumcision, is being engineered by men who are more concerned that you should show your zeal for God by what you do to your bodies, than that you should surrender your whole lives to the power and guidance of his Spirit. These men are simply out to save their own skins. They know, continues Paul, that they will be left in peace by the Jews so long as they advocate circumcision as proper Christian practice, whereas if they admit that Christ has opened up the way to God for Jews and Gentiles on equal terms without regard to Old Testament law, they will suffer the same persecution from their fellow-countrymen as he himself has done.

13–15. These agitators for circumcision, Paul goes on, are not really concerned about the divine nature of the Law of Moses. They do not even adhere to it strictly themselves. All they want is to be able to *boast* to the orthodox Jews that they have persuaded you to comply with this *outward rite*. As for me, says Paul, the only thing I want to boast about is that the Lord Jesus Christ died for me. My old life, my old outlook on everything is changed. Now I know that it matters not a whit whether I am a circumcised Jew or an uncircumcised Gentile. What matters is that through Christ I am a new man.

16. This, says the apostle, is the true Christian attitude, and may God's blessing rest upon all who subscribe to it, for they know that they are part of the *Israel of God*. Paul's great insight contained in these words, unique in the New Testament, shows his recognition of the major role that Israel in its long story had to play in the preparation for the gospel. Christianity is no new thing. It is the culmination both of God's choice of Abraham as the founding father of the People of God, and of the faith and moral standards of the Old Testament. We are caught up, as Christians, in God's plan for the salvation of the world within the framework of human history. It links us with Moses, Amos, and Isaiah, as much as with the twelve apostles and the saints who succeeded Paul.

17. Then in a final thrust at his opponents the apostle dares them to do their worst. They cannot win, for he is under the protection of Christ. It was a custom among the pagans, as the Galatians would well know, for those who were dedicated to the service of some god to be branded as a mark of their consecration and of their immunity from harm. Paul wryly refers to the scars on his own body—such as those that dated from the stoning he had suffered on his Galatian campaign (Acts 14: 19)—as the brand-marks that single him out as a man committed to Jesus through sharing his sufferings. Well might the apostle be called 'Paul the dauntless'.

18. The letter ends with a benediction and with a friendly word to his Galatian *brothers*. ✳

✳ ✳ ✳ ✳ ✳ ✳ ✳ ✳ ✳ ✳ ✳ ✳ ✳ ✳ ✳ ✳ ✳ ✳ ✳ ✳

THE MESSAGE OF GALATIANS FOR TODAY

Paul and the Church

Having worked our way through this letter, let us try now to see what it has to say to us today. An important element is the contribution that the epistle has to make to our knowledge of Paul himself. We have seen how closely the autobiographical information he gives us tallies with the account that Luke, Paul's devoted companion and the careful historian of his missionary journeys, gives us in the book of Acts. What Paul tells us in Galatians strengthens our confidence in the substantial accuracy of Acts, and fills in Luke's masterly summary of the early story of the Church with vivid personal details.

More than that, the letter helps us to see more clearly the real greatness of Paul as a man, to learn something more of the secret of his amazing success as virtually the creator of western Christendom, and to understand better his power of awakening loyalty and affection among his converts throughout the Church. On every page of the epistle we have seen evidence not only of a man with a brilliant mind, a trenchant controversialist, a fearless fighter, but of a man whose life was 'hidden with Christ in God' (Col. 3: 3). Paul was devoted to Christ, and it was this love that was turned outwards in care and concern for all Christ's people whom the apostle loved as if they were his own children.

It was this very fact that for Paul, ever since his experience on the Damascus road, Christ was the beginning and the end of everything, that determined his attitude to every problem that confronted him in the course of his missionary activities. The particular issue that he is dealing with in this letter was, as has been noted, vital for the whole future of the Church. If Paul had surrendered on this point, it would have meant the end of the Church as we know it, or rather as Paul knew it and as we hope and believe it will be once again.

For Paul the idea of a divided Church was unthinkable, and the real battle that he is fighting in this letter is to maintain the unity of the Body of Christ. If the Jewish Christians, in Galatia and elsewhere, had won the day, the Church would have been split into those congregations which counted themselves Christian by virtue of their acceptance of Christ and baptism, and those which maintained that circumcision and other features of Mosaic Law were essential additional qualifications for membership.

Paul could have argued his case on grounds of expediency, the necessity for a united Christian front against a pagan world, or some of the other pleas that are put forward today in favour of the reunion of the churches. He chose to fight, however, on basic principles. What constitutes a Christian? he asks, and gives the reply: Acceptance of Jesus Christ as Son of God and Saviour, and incorporation by baptism into the Israel of God, the Church. In the light of this, circumcision, an ancient and hallowed practice of deep significance which was part of Paul's own tradition, cannot be allowed to stand in the way of the unity of the church. By the same token, we have to ask ourselves today whether acceptance of papal infallibility, episcopal order, congregational independence, particular views on the Scriptures or the Atonement, adult baptism or infant baptism, seven sacraments or none, can be regarded as in any sense the ultimate criteria by which we recognize men and women as full and equal members of the Body of Christ.

The ultimate criterion of membership is commitment to Christ, and if we take Paul's argument to its logical conclusion today, Quakers and Jesuits, Salvation Army and Eastern Orthodox, all practising their own traditions, are already fully incorporated into the Israel of God. It may well be doubted whether in the last resort Paul would not have equated baptism with circumcision, as being a significant rite but not essential to salvation. His reasoning leads us, in the present state of a divided Church, to a full and formal acknowledgment of the validity of each other's traditions as the way to organic unity, rather than insistence on certain criteria of ministry and sacraments which cannot on Paul's view be regarded as anything more than accidents of history.

Faith and freedom

But it is in dealing with men as persons that this letter has most to say to us today. Behind the issue of circumcision and obedience to the Law of Moses, lies Paul's conviction about the nature of the Christian life. It is above all a personal relationship with Christ within the fellowship of his Church which expresses itself in the service of the community. If Paul was sure of anything, it was that his experience on the Damascus road had changed his whole life. This was the basis of all his subsequent thinking, the pivot round which all his activity revolved. What had happened to him when Christ 'took hold' of him then (Phil. 3 : 12) put everything in a new perspective.

As a devout and zealous Pharisee he had been trying all his life to come to terms with God. His upbringing and training had taught him to believe that by rigid compliance with the rules for behaviour laid down in the divinely appointed Law of Israel, he would know the inward peace that comes from being at one with God. He found that not only could he not comply with these exacting standards, but that even the high level of moral excellence which he did achieve left him dissatisfied and conscious of deep failure.

How could he bridge the gulf between his own imperfection and the perfection of God? How could he reach the point where at least he could say that he saw the beginning of the answer? As he searched his conscience with unflinching honesty, Paul admitted defeat. No amount of effort on his part to pull himself up to God could counteract the downward pull of self-interest, spiritual pride and human vanity. Only God himself could make us his sons and daughters as we were meant to be, and this he had now done through his own unique Son, Jesus Christ.

Paul is no dry-as-dust theologian. He is more of a poet or an impressionist painter. We therefore ought not to press too hard any words he uses in this letter or elsewhere to express his conviction that God has opened a new door for mankind. Left to himself, man is at odds with himself and the world. He knows this whenever he begins to think seriously about himself and is not content to live like a cabbage. But the good news that Paul devoted his life to proclaiming is that God has *not* left man to himself. He has come down to our level in the person of his Son, Jesus Christ, to lift us up to himself.

Christ became man not only to set us an example of how life should be lived, or in his teaching to leave us guidance for our attitude to one another, but to take the burden of our guilt and failure on his own shoulders. God in Christ identified himself with us by becoming one of us, by entering into our experience of human weakness and limitation, of suffering and death. But that is not the end of the story. The end of the story is not Good Friday but Easter Day. Christ faced all the things that separate us from God and defeated them all on our behalf. The gulf between God and man has been bridged by God himself. No one less than God could do it.

So Paul would say to us that the first step in the Christian life is to recognise that no amount of effort on our own part— trying to live up to any code of behaviour—will bring us into the right relationship with God or with our fellow men. The next step is to accept simply and gratefully that Christ does it for us. By committing ourselves to him, acknowledging him as our Lord and Saviour, pledging ourselves to his service, which is faith, we are no longer slaves to rules, slaves to fear of the unknown, slaves to fate, or slaves to ourselves, which is freedom.

Faith means freedom, says Paul, and then goes on quickly to the sequel. Freedom is not another name for individualism. We shall never find any encouragement for solitary Christianity in the apostle's writings. Whatever we may say or think about the failure of the Church to be what Jesus meant it to be, or what Paul tried to make it, it is clear that both the Master and his greatest disciple did not think of the Christian life except in terms of community. What Jesus did made Christian freedom possible; what he still does in the Church makes it a reality.

It is the power of the Holy Spirit, God's gift to the Church at Pentecost, that has enabled it to survive despite the abysmal failure of ourselves and every generation that has preceded us to represent Christ to the world. The Spirit of God is mightily offered there, in word, sacrament and fellowship, and when we are not too obsessed with our own concerns we recognize thankfully the supernatural resources that are available to help us.

Despite Paul's attack on the Law in this letter, he has to admit that there is a supreme law for all Christians, the law of love. There is nothing inconsistent in this with the claim that Christianity makes us free. As Paul has shown us, the essence of the Christian life is a spontaneous response to God's love as revealed in Jesus. Part of that response is faith, our offering of ourselves to Christ; but of equal importance is our offering of ourselves to others, to 'work for the good of all' (6: 10).

✳   ✳   ✳   ✳   ✳   ✳   ✳   ✳   ✳   ✳   ✳   ✳   ✳

INDEX

94

INDEX

For Reference

Not to be taken from this room